Brothers and Sisters of Disabled Children

Brothers and Sisters of Disabled Children

Peter Burke

Jessica Kingsley Publishers
London and Philadelphia

First published in the United Kingdom in 2004
by Jessica Kingsley Publishers
116 Pentonville Road
London N1 9JB, UK
and
400 Market Street, Suite 400
Philadelphia, PA 19106, USA

www.jkp.com

Library of Congress Cataloging in Publication Data
A CIP catalog record for this book is available from the Library of Congress

British Library Cataloguing in Publication Data
A CIP catalogue record for this book is available from the British Library

ISBN 978 1 84310 043 0

For Heather, my most strenuous supporter,
and our children, Marc, Sammy and Joe

Contents

LIST OF FIGURES   8

LIST OF TABLES   8

Introduction   9

Chapter 1   Theory and Practice   11

Chapter 2   A Framework for Analysis: The Research Design   29

Chapter 3   The Impact of Disability on the Family   41

Chapter 4   Family and Sibling Support   53

Chapter 5   Children as Young Carers   67

Chapter 6   Change, Adjustment and Resilience   77

Chapter 7   The Role of Sibling Support Groups   91

Chapter 8   Support Services and Being Empowered   105

Chapter 9   Conclusions: Reflections on Professional
Practice for Sibling and Family Support   119

Chapter 10   Postscript   129

APPENDIX 1   QUESTIONNAIRE: SUPPORT FOR BROTHERS
AND SISTERS OF DISABLED CHILDREN   131

APPENDIX 2   QUESTIONNAIRE: SIBLING GROUP EVALUATION   137

REFERENCES   141

SUBJECT INDEX   151

AUTHOR INDEX   157

List of Figures

Figure 1.1 Disability by association   26

Figure 2.1 The research design   36

List of Tables

Table 2.1 Reactive behaviours   33

Table 4.1 Parental views of the benefits of having a disabled child
           compared with their perceptions of siblings' caring
           responsibilities   59

Table 4.2 Family contact with formal and informal social networks   60

Table 4.3 Professional involvement and service provision
           (for sibling group)   61

Introduction

The inspiration for the research on which this book is based resulted from a conversation with my daughter. In a discussion about nothing in particular, one comment hit me with its crystal certainty. At the age of 10 my daughter reassured me about my disabled son's future in this way. She said: 'Don't worry daddy, when you are too old I will look after Marc.' Marc is her brother. He has a condition referred to as spastic quadriplegia, and severe learning disabilities. These labels do not really represent Marc as we know him, but it helps with the image of his dependency and the reason why his sister understood that his care needs were in many ways different from her own. My daughter's comment made me realise that it was not only I who was aware of my son's disabilities, but my daughter also, and she was thinking of his future at a time when my partner and I were 'taking a day at a time'. The inspiration drawn from that comment helped formulate a plan of research into the needs of siblings, and subsequently this book.

The book is structured to inform the practitioners (whether they are from the health, welfare or educational sectors), of the needs of siblings. I trust too, that the views expressed, based as they are on the experience of others and with some insights drawn from personal experience, will resonate with families in situations similar to my own.

Outline of chapters

Throughout the text quotations from families will be used to clarify points and issues raised, and detailed case examples will show how siblings react to the experience of living with a disabled brother or sister, creating 'disability by association'.

Chapter 1 provides an introduction and a theoretical framework for analysis linking to the key concepts: inclusion, neglect, transitions and adjustments, children's rights and finding a role for the practitioner. Models of disability are discussed to illustrate some of the differences found between professions. Figure 1.1 illustrates the process of developing disability by association. Chapter 2 introduces, in Part 1, a theoretically informed research typology (Table 2.1) which identifies a range of sibling behaviours as reactions to the experience of living with disability. In Part 2, the research design (Figure 2.1) and methods used are examined in some detail.

Chapter 3 is concerned with life at home. The impact of disability on the family and siblings introduces some of the difference between parental perceptions and sibling expectations. Chapter 4 looks at change, adjustments and resilience. The chapter illustrates how siblings' experience changes as they get older, at home and at school, and explores how the everyday restrictions and experiences create difficulties with making friends at school and in social group encounters.

Chapter 5 is concerned with children as young carers: what it means, how it makes life too restrictive. Chapter 6 examines different family experiences linked to a range of disability, and considers how family support may be provided.

Chapter 7 evaluates the use of a siblings support group and explains how such a group may meet the sibling's need for attention and also allow time for themselves. Chapter 8 is about support services, the need for personal empowerment and establishing a role for professionals.

Chapter 9 draws the various themes which inform the earlier chapters together and clarifies the role for professional practice. Chapter 10 adds a postscript, concerning disability by association, reflecting on some incidental and personal experiences gained shortly after concluding the research on which the book is based.

Chapter 1

Theory and Practice

In this chapter I will introduce a theoretical structure that will help to explain the need for working with siblings of children with disabilities. This builds on the idea that disability within one family member affects the whole family to such an extent that the family may feel isolated from others, or different because of the impact of disability. The impact of disability, as I will demonstrate, often has an initially debilitating and, often, continuing consequence for the whole family; I refer to this as 'disability by association'.

The incidence of disability within families is reported by the Joseph Rowntree Foundation to exceed 300,000 children in England and Wales (http://www.jrf.org.uk/knowledge, access findings report N79, 1999), which equates to 30 per 1,000. It is estimated that within an average health authority of 500,000 people, 250 families are likely to have more than one child with disabilities. According to Atkinson and Crawford (1995), some 80 per cent of children with disabilities have non-disabled siblings. The research I carried out indicated that siblings who experience disabilities within their families are to varying degrees disabled by their social experience at school and with their peers.

The sense of difference which disability imparts is partly explained by Wolfensberger (1998, p.104) with reference to devalued people, who, due to a process referred to as 'image association', are portrayed in a negative way; this happens when disabled people are stereotyped as 'bad'. For example, the image of Captain Hook, the pirate from J. M. Barrie's *Peter*

Pan, puts a disabled person in a wicked role; the image of Richard III in Shakespeare's play conveys badness associated with an individual whose twisted humped back was in reality a deformity invented by the Tudors to discredit his name. Not all disabled people will experience such an extreme sense of difference, but an element of 'bad' and 'disabled' may well be part of a stereotypical view of others: disability becomes, consequently, an undesirable social construct.

Living with disability may make a family feel isolated and alone, especially if social encounters reinforce the view that a disabled person is somehow 'not worthy'. Another family may acknowledge difference as a welcomed challenge, confirming individuality and a sense of being special, but the obstacles to overcome may be considerable.

Unfortunately, the feeling of 'image association' in a negative sense will often pervade the whole family and, whatever way they accommodate negative perceptions, such experiences are not restricted to those with disabilities themselves. Devaluing experiences are common to other disadvantaged groups, as Phillips (1998, p.162) indicates, 'children who are disabled, black, adopted or fostered can be stigmatised and labelled because they are different'. Disability is one area of possible disadvantage; race, class and gender are others, none of which I would wish to diminish by concentrating on disability. The case example of Rani and Ahmed (Chapter 4) demonstrates that ethnic differences combined with disability in the family compounds the experience of disability by association due to the nature of social experiences. Disability in children becomes a family experience, one which, as I shall show, has a particular impact on siblings.

Sibling perceptions

Siblings are caught up in a sense of being different within their family: disability becomes an identifying factor of difference from others, and as children, siblings may have difficulty when encountering their peers, who will ask questions like, 'Why are you the lucky one in your family?' This reinforces a sense of difference when the reality is that no child should question their 'luck' simply because of their similarity with others; the difference in terms of 'luck' here is equated with not being the disabled child of the family. Here, 'difference' is a subtle projection of the view point of the family 'with disabled children' as a 'disabled family' which, by the very act of questioning a non-disabled sibling, peers (probably unintentionally) reinforce what becomes a sense of disability by association, in essence, by the mere fact of belonging to a family that has a child with a perceived disability.

Disability and siblings

This book looks at how such differences may begin to be identified, with their various manifestations, forms and guises. It will seem that disability is being viewed here in a negative sense and, although that is not the intention, it may often be the reality of the experience of disabled people. The position of disabled people should be, as exemplified by Shakespeare and Watson (1998, p.24):

> Disabled people, regardless of impairment, are first and foremost human beings, with the same entitlements and citizenship rights as anyone else. It is up to society to ensure that the basic rights of disabled people are met within the systems and structures of education, transport, housing, health and so forth.

It is a fact that disabled people experience less than their rights and that this affects their families; it is why statements like the one above have to emphasise the rights of disabled people as citizens. The impact of disability is also felt within the family; to help this understanding, an examination of the medical and social model of disability will be made. These models are used to reflect on family experience, including the sibling immersion and understanding of disability, simply illustrated by the 'lucky' question above. The book itself is also informed by a rather brief, near concluding comment, in another (Burke and Cigno 2000, p.151). The text states: 'Being a child with learning disabilities is not easy. Neither is being a carer, a brother or a sister of such a child.' The implication of the second sentence was written prior to the comment from my daughter, mentioned in the Introduction, when she expressed the view that she would care for her disabled brother when I was too old to do so. It needed the personal, combined with my earlier research evidence, to achieve this focus on the needs of siblings. What the quote above demonstrates is the power of the written word to lie dormant, but language in its expressive form reflects on the reality of experience and, like disability itself, the consequences may be unexpected, not even realised or particularly sought, until a spark of insight may begin an enquiry and raise the need to ask a question about the way of things. In this case, the question is, 'What it is like to be a sibling of a disabled brother or sister?' This book is based on the need to answer that question.

The context of learning disability, mentioned above, is necessarily broadened here to include disability as the secondary experiences of brothers and sisters who share part of their home lives with a sibling with disabilities. This is not intended to diminish, in any sense, the needs of individuals with learning disabilities, but it is helpful for the initiation of an examination of the situation of siblings whose brothers or sisters are identified, diagnosed or labelled in some way as being disabled.

Parents may understand the needs of siblings as they compete for their share of parental attention, yet older siblings may share in the tasks of looking after a younger brother or sister. The siblings of a disabled brother or sister, as demonstrated by my research (Burke and Montgomery 2003), will usually help with looking after their brother or sister who is disabled, even when they are younger than them. In gaining this experience siblings are different from 'ordinary' siblings. Indeed, parental expectations may in fact increase the degree of care that is required by siblings when they help look after a brother or sister with disabilities, irrespective of any age difference.

The expectation of every child is that they should be cared for, and experience some form of normality in family life. The situation of siblings is that the experience and interaction with a brother or sister is for life unless some unfortunate circumstance interrupts that expectation. Brothers and sisters will often have the longest relationship in their lives, from birth to death. It is partly because of this special relationship that in my research bid to the Children's Research Fund I was keen to explore the situation of siblings of disabled children.

The original research report, produced for the Children's Research Fund, was called, *Finding a Voice: Supporting the Brothers and Sisters of Children with Disabilities* (Burke and Montgomery 2001b). This text was later published in a revised form for the BASW *Expanding Horizons* series (Burke and Montgomery 2003) to enable practitioners to access the findings as submitted to the funding body. This book is a more fully developed examination of detail arising from that report, citing case examples not previously published and providing more comprehensive information on the families and young people involved.

In a Parliamentary Question raised in the House of Lords the Rt Hon. Lord Morris of Manchester was concerned that some form of action to support siblings of children with disabilities should be taken by the Government, this following his reading of the original report (Burke and Montgomery 2001b). In a written reply from Baroness Blackstone on 27 March 2001 reference was made to the Government's *Quality Protects: Framework for Action* programme, with its £885 million support, suggesting that this would improve children's services. The *Framework for the Assessment of Children in Need and their Families* (Department of Health 2000a) was also mentioned, which stressed 'the importance of the relationship between disabled children and their siblings'. However, the needs of siblings remain to be fully understood within the framework, and this text clarifies some of the suggestions identified in the original report (Burke and Montgomery 2001b), indicating that the guidance provided within the assessment framework is incomplete with regard to the needs of sibling's of children with disabilities.

Rights and individualism

Although I will draw attention to the current legislation in Britain, the ethics governing professional practice is underpinned by the United Nations Convention on the Rights of the Child (1989), which requires that rights apply to *all children* without discrimination (article 2) and that children have the right to express an opinion in any matter relating to them, which is a basic entitlement to freedom of expression (article 12). When these rights are balanced with the child's right to dignity, the promotion of self-reliance and the right of children with disabilities to enjoy a full and decent life, we adopt an inclusive entitlement framework. Also, all children should have the right to an education, based on an equal opportunity premise and enabling the realisation of their fullest potential (article 28, 29): any factors which deny these entitlements is a breach of a child's right. In this text I intend documenting the situation of siblings so that something may be done to improve their situation in line with the Convention ratified in the UK in 1991 (Centre for Inclusive Education, http://inclusion.uvve.ac.uk/csie/unscolaw.htm, 2003).

My research with my colleague (Burke and Montgomery 2001) was concerned with family experience and particularly that of siblings of children with disabilities. I have already indicated that the experience of siblings at home differs through additional caring responsibilities, but that difference may lead siblings also to experience discrimination at school or in the neighbourhood through living in a family with a disabled child (Burke and Montgomery 2003). Here I seek to explain in more detail the experiences of siblings to show whether this experience is due to difference, disability or discrimination. The intention is to help the experience to be understood and, should it infringe against the fundamental rights of the child, it is to be hoped that a professional or indeed a family member will recognise it as such and take action to uphold the rights of the child concerned. Action in this case means challenging the assumption that discrimination against an individual on the grounds of disability, or indeed for reasons of race, gender or class, is unacceptable.

The sense of being different which is generated as a consequence of disability is important to understand, because disability can often result from the expressive perceptions and actions of others who attach the label of 'disability' to individuals who might otherwise not consider themselves disabled or in any way different. Some may wish to be identified as different, which is their right, but difference which is imposed by others is potentially discriminating no matter how well intentioned. In an interview for the Disability Rights Commission a disabled actor explained that he sees 'disability' as a social construct, one carrying entirely negative connotations. Since he 'came out' as disabled, he sees this as a struggle against an oppressive society (http://www.drc-gb.org/drc/default.asp, 2003).

It appears that his view of his disability is that it is caused by the perceptions of other rather than his own sense of being disabled. In a discussion with a woman who was mildly disabled the same actor asked if she had ever been made aware of discrimination because of her disability.

The woman replied that, although the thought had occurred to her, she wasn't really sure. The actor concluded that, although she had succeeded in getting on with her life, inside she must have known that she was being pitied and not treated properly. (http://www.drc-gb.org/drc/InformationAndLegislation/ NewsRelease_020904.asp, 2003).

This view represents a socialising form of disability, which is discussed in the following part of this chapter under 'Models of disability', but here the message is that a socially stigmatising perception of disability exists, whether as the result of pity or some other emotion, and socially constructs disability. Where disability is socially constructed, as mentioned by Shakespeare and Watson (1998, p.24) it is society's responsibility to demolish that construction. Oliver (1996, p.33) in expressing the view of the Union of the Physically Impaired Against Segregation (UPIAS) is keen to express the group's view that disability is 'imposed upon individuals' in addition to the impairment experienced by the disabled person themselves: in other words, it is an additional barrier which is oppressive and socially excluding. The attitudinal barrier, as it may be conceived, may also extend to siblings and non-disabled family members, so that a secondary disability is socially constructed, which is the product of the power of negative perceptions. The need to change such perceptions at a social level is imperative, so that being different does not lead to attitudinal oppressions or result in physical barriers or restrictions.

Clearly, there is a need for a broader policy requirement to initiate the removal of physical barriers combined with a social education for us all. This will necessarily include the adaptation of restricting areas: changing attitudinal barriers to treating people as people first and as citizens with equal rights (but perhaps with differing levels of need depending on the impairment experienced which should be met without charge or censure).

Models of disability

There are two models of disability with which I am mainly concerned: the first is called the 'medical' model and the second, the 'social' model of disability. It is important to understand these two models because they help to clarify differences in professional perceptions, although, it has to be said, models are just that: not the reality of experience, but a means towards understanding, in these examples, the experiences of people with disabilities.

The medical model (Gillespie-Sells and Campbell 1991) views disability as a condition to be cured, it is pathological in orientation and 'consequently' is indicative that a person with disabilities has a medical problem that has to be remedied. This portrays the disabled person as having a problem or condition which needs putting right and this is usually achieved by following some form of treatment, which may be perfectly acceptable in a patient–doctor relationship when it is the patient who is seeking treatment. It is, however, questionable when the patient is not seeking treatment, but because of a disability may be expected to go for medical consultations to monitor their condition when this may achieve little or nothing. Considering the individual only in treatment terms is to allow the pathological to override the personal, so that the person becomes an object of medical interest, the epileptic, the spastic quadriplegic, the deaf, dumb and blind kid who has no rights.

A social model, on the other hand, indicates that disability is exacerbated by environmental factors and consequently the context of disability extends beyond the individual's impairment. Physical and social barriers may contribute to the way disability is experienced by the individual (Swain et al. 1993). Questions may be asked, following the suggestions of Oliver (1990) such as, 'What external factors should be changed to improve this person's situation?' For example, the need for attendance at a special school might be questioned if there is a more inclusive alternative within the locality, which is preferable to assuming that the child with a disability must, necessarily, attend a special school. This is like saying that a disabled person must be monitored by a consultant rather than visiting their general practitioner when a need to do so, as with all of us, is thought advisable. Consequently, in the school example, mainstream education might be preferable for many or most children with disabilities, but is only viable if accompanied by participative policies of inclusion and encouragement for the child at school, together with classroom support. The social model should promote the needs of the individual within a community context in such a way that the individual should not suffer social exclusion because of his or her condition. In the example given, rather than withdrawing the child from the everyday experiences of others, integrated education would mean that he or she is part of the mainstream: it is a kind of normalisation process. The social model simply encourages changes to be made to the social setting so that the individual with some form of impairment is not disadvantaged to the point of being disabled by situational, emotional and physical barriers to access.

The world, however, is not so simplistically divided, for where the doctor cannot cure, surgery can at times alter some elements of the disability, by, for example, operations to improve posture and mobility, although 'the need' for major surgery may provoke controversial reactions (see Oliver 1996). One view expressed by some people with physical disabilities is that a disabled person should not try to enter the 'normal world'. This reaction is a consequence of viewing medical progress as a way of overcoming disability by working on the individual with an impairment, who is made to feel abnormal and disabled, rather than viewing the impairment as a difference, which should be understood by those with no prior experience of the condition.

The first model assumes that people are disabled by their condition, the second by the social aspects of their experiences which give rise to feelings of difference that portray the individual as disabled. This locates disability not within the individual but in their interactions with the environment. In practice, the emphasis should rest between a careful assessment of personal circumstances in each individual case and a full consideration of the consequences of wider structural changes. The latter should benefit all people with impairments when accessing resources, which may be automatically allocated to meet the needs of the non-disabled majority. For example, in providing lifts for wheelchair access to multistorey buildings, ambulant people might not perceive a problem, while those in wheelchairs experience restrictions.

In brief, then, the medical model on the whole emphasises the person's medical condition, illness or disability as being different from the norm. The social model of disability tends to be holistic, placing the individual in his or her context and focusing on the duty of others to effect change, so that the behaviour of others and the opportunities offered do not promote a sense of disability as a condition to be discriminated against, ignored or avoided. Impairments should not of themselves be restrictive if barriers, attitudinal and physical, are eliminated. The medical and social models are not intended to represent a right or wrong way of looking at the world: both are limited, both have their place.

Identifying an integrated model

Some years ago I suggested reconstructing the social model (Burke 1993) to reflect a person-centred approach. This may be viewed as a contradiction in terms, given that the medical view is at the level of the personal and the social at the level of the community. The latter suggests that major societal changes are required to remove disability, but at the level of an individual impairment, personal assistance may be required. This is where the medical and social intersect, and planning is needed to work with people with disability, whether children, adults or siblings. This planning would be based on an assessment of need, which should assist the user to overcome any barriers or difficulties encountered through impairment, whether it be gaining access to buildings or resources or linking to barriers of a social, or attitudinal form. The necessary changes could be assisted by a worker who monitors and reviews any intended plan of action with the person concerned, changing the assessment as required according to the perceived needs of the individual involved, and effectively acting as a co-ordinator of resources in the process. This acknowledges the needs of the individual and, rather than focusing on the nature of the condition which is viewed as disabling, moves into the arena of social functioning. It accepts the idea that Oliver (1996) advocates, that disabled people need acceptance by society as themselves. It is limited, however, because acceptance does not challenge, may imply that disability is endured or put up with, so that the value base of others remains unchanged and a sense of disabled isolation may continue. However, if this social element of need were extended to include others' responsibility not to disable people by their reactions, but to undertake some form of social education to accept people with disabilities, then the model would at least provide a view of a need for change, by identifying what those changes should be.

The person-centred approach is basically interactive and recognises the reciprocal nature of relationships. Where children with disabilities are concerned, as with any other child, carers are also included in the assessment. A health practitioner needs to know about diagnosis and treatment and hence to focus on the pathological; the social worker needs to understand and have the skills to deal with individual and family difficulties or problems and so is less concerned with the medical condition, except in its impact on a person's ability to deal with the difficulty or problem. Social workers, too, through their training, possess networking and negotiating skills. Practitioners can learn from each other's perspectives. The medical practitioner needs to see individual needs beyond the physical: the social worker needs to take account of the meaning and effects of a debilitating condition.

The use of an integrated model shows that the medical and social approaches do not exist in isolation, but in reality overlap. Diagnosis is important from a parent's point of view, if they wish to put a name to their condition and understand whether others will be affected by it. Self-help groups might be formed for such needs, or organisations which address specific needs – for example, Mencap, Scope, etc. In many ways, parents feel that they cannot move forward unless a diagnosis is forthcoming, often placing doctors in a difficult situation where the case is uncertain (Burke and Cigno 1996). Nevertheless, because disability is not necessarily curable, in the traditional sense, it should not entail denial of the rights to citizenship and should avoid an association with judgements about ability and socially accepted standards of physical normality. A social perspective complements what should be the best medical service designed to help the child.

The social model of disability, when viewed from the perspective of others is based on ideas of 'social construction', where the concern is to do with changing a narrow social element, and considers the individual with disabilities as having a problem, without a ready-made solution. This is rather like the medical view, and needs to change to embrace ecological factors and to promote equality on an individual basis without seeing 'problems' within the ownership of the individual. The need is to revise the view that, although disability may exist at some level of physical restriction and inequality, this should not be so. A change in those attitudinal and social perceptions that equate disability with incapacity, inability or even as being ineffectual within everyday experiences, is needed to remove the stigma associated with disability. This is like a change from a disease-model of disability, similar to Wilton's (2000) concern about the disease-model of homosexuality, in which homosexuality is seen as a kind of medical illness rather than a state of being that must be socially recognised and accepted. Thus the social model of disability, as informed by Shakespeare and Watson's (1998, p.24) view, is that social experience is more about the interactive elements which define the individual's inherent needs, than a fixed state or condition that might be amenable to treatment. However, this view extends to those who are non-disabled and for whom the need to accept, understand and promote aid is a necessity.

The social model is not without its critics because its restricted vision excludes the importance of race and culture which, as Marks (1999) suggests, ignores an important element of personal constructs, amounting to the oppression of Black disabled people. The fact that disabled Black people experience multiple disadvantage amounts to a compounded sense of difference from an oppressive society (see the case of Rani and Ahmed in Chapter 4). Clearly, the need is for a positive view of disability, although the evidence from the research cited tends to accentuate the negative elements rather than a more desirable celebration of disability as contributing to the essence of humanity.

How the model translates to siblings

The integrated, person-centred model of disability as it might be called, and as discussed so far, relates, to state the obvious, to people with disabilities. The question then of interpreting such a model in terms of the siblings of children with disabilities has to be considered. Essentially when considering the social model the impact of an impairment should be reduced by an acceptance that factors which convey a sense of disability should be removed. In the social setting attitudes should promote acceptance of a person whether disabled or not, and in a physical sense too, barriers or obstacles should not be put in place which promote a sense of disability. However, the fact that disabled people still face obstacles of both a social and physical kind means that barriers to disability still exist.

In understanding the relationship of siblings to a brother or sister with disabilities the sense is that the 'disabling element' of the social model identifies environmental exclusion as partly resulting from limited physical accessibility to public places. Non-disabled people need to perceive such physical restrictions as not being the fault of the disabled person. However, the realities are such that disabled people feel blamed for their condition (Oliver 1990) and may view disability as a personal problem that must be overcome. In turn, siblings may perceive themselves as disabled by association, in being a relative, and having to confront the experience of exclusion or neglect as already faced by a disabled sibling. In effect, the experience of childhood disability becomes the property of the family as each member shares the experience of the other to some degree. In a perfect situation, where exclusion and neglect does not occur, then this model of disability would cease to exist because it would not help an understanding of the experience faced by the 'disabled' family as a unit.

If we are to deconstructing social disability then we need to remove the barriers to disability, whether attitudinal or physical. Fundamental to understanding the need for such a deconstruction are three concepts, which link with those identified by Burke and Cigno (2000), namely: neglect, social exclusion and empowerment. The first two convey a negative sense, the latter a positive approach which is construed as a necessary reaction to diminish the experience of neglect and exclusion.

Neglect

The term 'neglect' according to Turney (2000) is concerned, in social work at least, with the absence of care and may have physical and emotional connotations. Further, neglect is a normative concept (Tanner and Turney 2000) because it does not have a common basis of understanding; it means different things to different people. In any research, for example, into child protection neglect is a form of abuse in which a child is deprived of basic health and social needs. If neglect is present as might be understood from Turney's conception it relates to an absence or exclusion of care that parents should provide for their children. In the case of a child with disabilities the siblings may experience differential levels of care depending on the availability of the parents, which may not equate with the needs of those siblings, but equally may not be classified as neglect amounting to abuse. I define 'neglect' in this context as follows:

> Neglect is used to convey a form of social exclusion which may arise from a lack of understanding or awareness of need. This may be because individuals are ignorant of the needs of others. Here 'neglect' is used as a relative term concerning siblings who, compared with other members of the family, may receive differing levels of care and attention from their carers. In the latter case, neglect may be an omission caused by competing pressures rather than a deliberate act or intent.

Social exclusion

Exclusion is concerned with those on the margins of society, those who have an 'inability to participate effectively in economic, social political and cultural life' (Oppenheim 1998, p.13). Often exclusion is about the incapacity of individuals to control their lives, and it requires inclusive policies to bring about change, to provide an opportunity for each citizen 'to develop their potential' (Morris 2001, p.162). Indeed, as Middleton (1999) found, even the Social Exclusion Unit (http://www.social exclusionunit.gov.uk, 2003) failed to consider the needs of disabled children, as I too discovered when using their search engine that showed that no results were available; similarly 'siblings and disability' also found no records available within their database. It would seem that exclusion of children with disabilities is not a concept of which the Social Exclusion Unit has much understanding. This lack of recognition impacts on families with disabled children because participation with others in their daily lives is difficult in whatever form of relationship that takes, where an experience of potential exclusion may occur. Hence, the term 'exclusion' helps provide a benchmark when assessing the involvement of individuals within their daily activities. I define exclusion with regard to siblings as follows:

> Social exclusion is a deliberate prohibition or restriction which prevents a sibling from engaging in activities shared by others. It may be a form of oppression, as experienced when denying an individual his or her entitlement to express their views or a form of segregation when only individuals with certain characteristics are allowed to engage in

particular activities (restrictive attitudes or membership entitlement based on race being examples).

Empowerment

The idea of empowerment is pertinent to the situation of siblings of children with disabilities and disabled people generally: it is based on the need for making choices (Sharkey 2000), a basic right of consumers. Empowerment may include power, as a worker may empower, by enabling access to a service that is needed (Dowson 1997, p.105). However, when children have disabilities, parents and indeed, professionals might, understandably, tend to be more focused on the child with disabilities and not on the needs of siblings. The needs of sibling's should also be recognised as part of the family experience of living with disability and siblings should be included in whatever concerns their brother or sister. Empowerment is defined as follows:

> Empowerment is about enabling choices to be made and is vital to the needs of individuals, especially so, if an element of choice is lacking, as it will be for some family members due to exclusion or neglect, deliberate or not. The initial stage of empowerment requires individuals to be included in decisions which concern their needs. This represents the first stage of enabling the process of choice and freedom of access to begin.

The 'key terms', neglect, social exclusion and empowerment, were implicit in my pilot study (Burke and Montgomery 2001a), and now, following the research, I can clarify the sense behind this initial conceptual understanding. My prior concern was to promote the term 'social inclusion' rather than 'social exclusion' as defined above. This is because my research work revealed more 'social exclusion' than the polar opposite 'inclusion'. Indeed, the process of empowerment itself should seek to redress the position of exclusion by promoting an inclusive experience. This understanding enables us to begin to prescribe a role for welfare professionals, defining their task as enabling families to become included families – that is, helping family members to make choices from a range of support services. It certainly appears to be the case, as demonstrated by Burke and Cigno (1996), that most families welcome the offer of professional support.

Siblings also need to be included in discussions between parents and professional representatives, as indeed, do children with disabilities. Services are a basic requirement for the family, but families might need encouragement to secure them, and siblings, more often than not, might be excluded from elements of service provision, except when they have access to a siblings group or services designed to facilitate their needs.

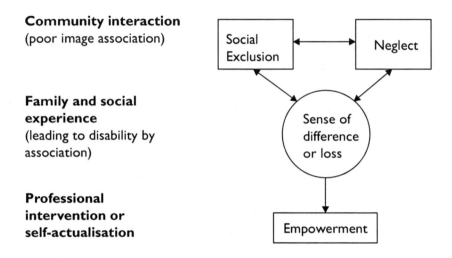

Community interaction
(poor image association)

Family and social experience
(leading to disability by association)

Professional intervention or self-actualisation

Figure 1.1 Disability by association

Disability by association

The model represented in Figure 1.1, represents the process of disability by association, reflecting the experience of neglect that siblings may face at home through the competing and overwhelming needs of a disabled sibling, which may then be compounded by experiences of social exclusion that exist away from home. The latter may be due to bad experiences at school, with friends or on social occasions, which in combination develop a sense of disability within the sibling, or disability by association. The sense is that disability is viewed by 'normal' people as different, which leads to a stigma associated with disability. When a person is stigmatised by disability then 'normal' people erect a barrier to exclude the 'infectiousness' of the perceived stigma. This means that associating with disability is likely to be transmitted to the normal world, and as such it is feared. The impact of this is probably a result of negatively conveyed social attitudes, which with a typical 'young carers' role at home must influence the sibling's concept of self with certain disadvantages compared with their peers. The escape route from the perception of disadvantage, or disability by association, is through some means of empowerment: that is, to gain a positive identity in relationships with others. The role of the sibling support group, reported on in Chapter 7 provides one way by which this may be achieved.

Chapter 2

A Framework for Analysis
The Research Design

This chapter examines the construction of typologies and the research design that enabled the differing experiences of siblings with a disabled brother or sister to be more clearly understood. The underlying thesis as developed in Chapter 1 is that siblings experience disability by association, because the experience of living with a disabled brother or sister, which will seem perfectly ordinary, will to some extent become a disabling experience for them, changes their lives as a consequence of this and because of interactive experiences away from home, at school, with friends and during outings with their family.

The model presented for making this examination reflects both positive and negative experience of a greater or lesser magnitude according to the experience recounted in interview, and builds on lessons learned from the pilot study (Burke and Montgomery 2001). Case examples will be linked to the framework throughout the book, to illustrate how disability by association impacts on the lives of siblings and on the family. Clearly, the experience of disabled children should be positively reinforced by encounters with others, but this is not the experience of disabled children or of their siblings. Positive experience should be the norm, but until attitudes are changed within the wider realms of society, the experience of disability discrimination within the context of childhood experience will continue.

This chapter is in two parts; the first part is about the development of typologies and shows how different theoretical models enabled the qualitative elements of the case material to be examined. The second is about the research design and will be particularly helpful to those with a desire to undertake studies of this type or who are just curious about how the fieldwork research was carried out.

Part 1: Developing a classification of family types

In order to aid the analysis of qualitative data derived from the interviews held with 22 families, it is helpful to clarify the framework on which this examination is based. This framework is really a model against which the main features of sibling experiences might be typified. It is derived from an examination of the locus of control, which is explained below, and bereavement stages which link to loss. The data from siblings is essentially a snapshot of the experiences reflected during interview, which is also informed by the survey questionnaire; bringing together both data of a quantitative kind with descriptive data from interview.

In simplifying the examination of the information available, high and low orders of reactions to disabled siblings are considered and demonstrated by their own accounts of their situation, and reactions may seem more highly charged for some compared with others – hence the high or low order. However, some siblings appear to experience little difference to their home life, and this non-reaction is described as compliance, a basic reaction which is underpinned by the psychology of interpersonal behaviour (Atkinson *et al.* 1990). The need to address issues for siblings may be aided by examining the 'locus of control', which is a relatively simple way of determining the functional nature of decision-making within the family.

The locus of control

The locus of control (Lefcourt 1976) may be used in cognitive-behavioural therapy (Burke 1998). It provides a framework for the assessment of any situation that requires understanding and some form of action. I provided examples of its usefulness in the field of children with learning disabilities in Burke (1998), but to recap: control is viewed as either internal or external. Individuals who take responsibility for their own actions and see consequences as a result of their own efforts are said to have an internal locus of control. Those who see situations and outcomes as outside their influence and who believe that their lives are subject to the control of others have an external locus of control.

Understanding the world of the child helps to identify family situations from a child's view, and in so doing aids our determination of reasonable and realistic goals. Children with disabilities are often very dependent on others (but not necessarily so) and thus have an external locus of control. Behavioural interventions, as well as other kinds, need to recognise this, but putting it into practice requires some means of redirecting and reinforcing desired behaviours that are within the individual's control. Experience of success or failure (Meadows 1992) may influence the locus of control; those that succeed reinforce an internal locus, while those that fail tend to be more fatalistic, and situations will be viewed as beyond control. The aim of intervention should be to increase the child's repertoire of skills and choices, enabling a move towards positive self-determination and independence appropriate to their age.

The locus is discussed with particular emphasis in relation to Fay and her support for her disabled brother Michael (see Chapter 6) and is identified in Table 2.1 (5) which shows Fay's highly positive reaction to her brothers' needs. Fay's experience is also indicative of her own stigmatisation by school children, displaying disability by association. In order to understand the adjustments that children like Fay experience, reference to the stages in the bereavement process is helpful in explaining some typical reactions.

Stages in bereavement

Understanding of the adjustment which needs to be made to accomodate the effects of stress is aided by Kübler-Ross (1969), who classified the process of adjustment followed by individuals who reacted to the experience of bereavement. Bereavement follows the loss of a loved one and will trigger reflections about missed opportunities; such reflections can be both painful and pleasurable for the bereaved individual. Other models of grief reactions include Parkes (1975) and Worden (1991). All are concerned with individual reactions to bereavement as a significant event, and it is suggested that, although all changes do not promote a bereavement reaction, the accumulation of stress resulting from home circumstances for a sibling of a brother or sister with a disability, may in some, if not all cases, produce reactions which are similar to the bereavement process.

Kübler-Ross identified five major reactive stages to bereavement: denial, anger, guilt, depression and acceptance. In order to achieve some form of adjustment, a person who is bereaved has to come to terms with their experience. There is a sense of working through each of the stages to achieve a level of acceptance. This mirrored a major theme which emerged from my interviews with siblings of brothers and sisters with disabilities – that they adjusted to different experiences, not especially at home, but at school and with their peers and friends. It seems that different experiences become stressing when the experience is out of the ordinary, but this is dependent on the resilience of the individual to accommodate change (see Chapter 6). The stage of depression identified by Kübler-Ross (1969) is not used as part of a sibling reaction because, following interviews, it emerged that 'protection' was a more representative term for the type of reaction that followed the experience of living with childhood disability. The sense too, is not of a linear progression through five stages of reaction; it is more likely to be an adaptation to a particular form of reaction that is identified, fitting a similar finding in my earlier work (Burke and Cigno 1996) which examined the need for family support and identified specific family response types. However, although it suggests a degree of 'fixation' according to the behavioural type identified, this is not to say that the characteristics are not amenable to change, and each confers some degree of advantage and disadvantage for the child concerned.

In Table 2.1 a typology of reactive behaviours adopted by siblings is identified and each is explored within the subsequent chapters. All names used are invented to protect the identity of the child; also, some minor changes are made to case detail for reasons of confidentiality. In Table 2.1 (1) the negative reaction of Jane represents an extreme case because she emulated a 'feigned' disability, apparently to reaffirm her position within the family – she got more attention. Her reaction seems compatible with an internalised anger and an ability to express it. The interactive experiences

Table 2.1 Reactive behaviours			
Typical behaviour identified following interview	**Locus of control** from Lefcourt (1976)	**Stage of adjustment** based on Kübler-Ross (1969)	**Example & location**
1. Negative reaction (high)	internal	anger	Jane & Richard (Ch.3) Douglas & Harry (Ch.3) Rani & Ahmed (Ch.4) Rachel & Susan (Ch.8)
2. Negative reaction (low)	external	denial	John, James & Harry (Ch.3)
3. Compliant behaviour (see Atkinson *et al.* 1985)	external	guilt	Joe, David & Daniel (Ch.4) Alan & Mary (Ch.6) Peter & Ian (Ch.7)
4. Positive reaction (low)	internal	protection	Jenny, Paul & Victoria (Ch.6)
5. Positive reaction (high)	external	accepting	Fay & Michael (Ch.5) Robert & Henry (Ch.6)

of children mixing with other children may reinforce a negative or positive identity, but a number find such experiences disabling, and Jane's 'disability' may in part be a reaction to the stresses imposed by other children; her disability then becomes a form of escape. The locus of control will help to decide where control might be initiated. The reality for most individuals is probably a mixture of internal and external control, which to some degree determines the type of behaviour followed, whether internal or externally controlled.

These observations are based on my professional judgement concerning each case and the need to formulate a problem-solving strategy once the reaction is understood. This is a dependence on expert judgement, which fits within Bradshaw's (1993) division of social needs, where normative need is determined by professional interpretation. Clearly, there is some element of subjective bias in my categorising behaviours although the qualitative reflection of individual reactions across the range of behaviours reported has validity (Mayntz *et al.* 1976) for practice in the health, welfare and educational fields. The thesis concerning disability by association clarifies the reaction type reported, indicating, as clarified by Mayntz *et al.* (1976), that the approach is a valid mechanism for analysis (see research design comments in Part 2 of this chapter).

In these examples the experience of a non-disabled sibling confirms the reality of disability as part of the family experience. The experience of siblings is identified as 'disability by association', and siblings experience a variety of reactions to their identification with disability, whether seeking attention from professional and familial sources or minimising its impact to draw less attention to themselves. Further examples will illustrate a positive reactive type (developed from the theory of resilience: see Rutter 1995), and a negative reactive type, which is partly a form of passive compliance (the acceptance of disability through conformity to family pressures, based on the theory of compliance). The nature of reactions to disability tends to confer 'disability by association', because non-disabled siblings experience a sense of being disabled, a factor which is illustrated throughout the remaining chapters in this text, following an examination of the research design.

Part 2: The research design

This text presents a mainly qualitative account of the research which was initially based on a survey design. The exclusion of endless tables is deliberate and is intended to retain, as far as possible, a reader-friendly text suitable for interpretation for practice within the welfare professions. The quantitative data were derived from 74 variables, which enabled analysis and are identified on the survey questionnaire in bold type (Appendix 1). The survey data are supported by case studies to improve the reliability of the research. Cross-tabulations of the survey data were performed to test for associations with only a few significant tables being selected for inclusion within the text, and these were of some importance regarding an earlier finding which suggested (i) a number of families existed in relative isolation from any form of support, (ii) isolated families received less support than others whose needs might not be so great, and (iii) siblings acted as informal carers for their disabled siblings. Non-significant data are, nevertheless, also of importance in field research of this type as Goda and Smeeton (1993) recognise. 'Non-significant' is not synonymous with 'irrelevance' or indeed proof that an association does not exist and may only be a reflection of a limited database.

The research was conducted in four stages; the pilot study, the main stage survey based on children attending a siblings support group, the third stage involving interviews with parents and the final stage interviews with children at a children's centre. The main stage featured a control group of families not attending a siblings support group and included one follow-up family interview (see Figure 2.1).

A research assistant and I conducted interviews, both of us having carried out a number of such interviews on previous occasions. In total, 56 families completed questionnaires during the main stage of the study, with 177 children between them – nearly three children per family. The ages of children with disabilities ranged from 2 to 18 years with a mean of 8 years; and sibling's ages varied from birth to 30 years with a mean of 13 for girls and 14 for boys. The ratio of girl to boy siblings was a little under 2 to 1, a feature which might inform the nature of caring activities undertaken by siblings, given a gender bias. Twenty-two families were randomly selected for interview together with 24 of the family's children.

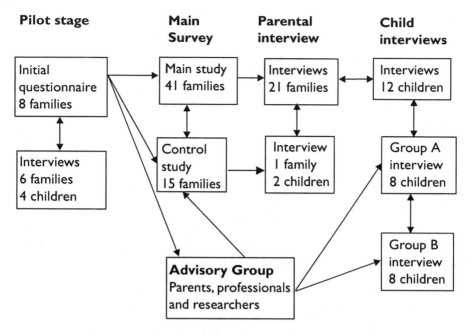

Figure 2.1 The research design

Research involving children

Although permission was sought from both parents and the children concerned with the research, the question of whether such research should be undertaken needs qualification. Beresford (1997) puts forward two arguments against involving children in research: first, the belief that children cannot be sources of valid data; and second, that there is a danger of exploiting children. Such objections were countered by Fivush *et al.* (1987), who showed that children are capable of reporting matters accurately and that it is adults who misrepresent the data they provide (see also McGurk and Glachan 1988). Indeed, Morris (1998) points out that disabled children and young people are rarely consulted or involved in decisions that concern them, although the research process reported here demonstrates the value of interviewing young people and shows that they have opinions and views on matters not only concerning themselves but their families also. The process of seeking permission is viewed as protecting the children from any possible exploitation, as indeed is my own professional responsibility as both a social worker and academic researcher.

Stages in the research

The pilot study involved ten families; eight families completed the initial questionnaire, and four siblings were interviewed; initial results were reported in Burke and Montgomery (2001a). The families were each sent a self-completion questionnaire and within it was a request to gain access to the families, providing they agreed, and a further request for permission to interview a sibling. Siblings were not interviewed without the agreement of the families and the siblings themselves could withdraw from the interview if they so wished, even if this was at the point of undertaking the interview: none did. Interviews were held at home.

The families who were sent the pilot questionnaire were identified through a local family centre; all were asked before the questionnaire was distributed if they would mind helping with the initial stage of the research. All agreed, although two of the ten did not return the question-naire, and only half of those who did (four) agreed that their children might participate in a face-to-face follow-up interview. I noted that the four refusals to allow children to be interviewed were linked to children who were under the age of 8 years, but I also thought that younger children might have some difficulties in communicating their ideas – indeed, that I might not possess the necessary skills to make correct inter-pretations of their views or ideas. Moreover, I did not wish to draw attention to the presence of disability within the family, should siblings not understand or even realise, that their brother or sister was considered 'disabled' by others. Consequently, I felt that our main study should mainly concern children over the age of 8.

As well as accessing families and children where permission was granted, the pilot questionnaire tested the feasibility of the questionnaire itself as a research instrument – basically the pilot study was a check on the validity of the research instrument (Corbetta 2003, p.82), to ensure it was testing what it was intended to test regarding the experience of siblings. In the original design of the questionnaire the number of questions asked extended to six pages, which seemed excessive, given the comments of the respondents that some simplification and reduction of the questions was required. Part of one question was not answered at all; it asked 'Do your non-disabled children help you with the care of their disabled brother or sister?' and was followed by a 'yes' or 'no' category, with further spaces to qualify the 'yes' or 'no'. There was no qualification of not caring responses, while the affirmative caring response elicited a series of responses related to the caring task, for example, 'fetches (name) clothing when asked'. Removing the 'no' category and similar reductions resulted in the questionnaire in Appendix 1, reducing the overall questionnaire to four pages. The self-completed pilot questionnaire was also used as a basis for interviewing parents and the children involved. This pattern of interview succeeding the survey questionnaire was followed through in the main survey and interview stages of the research.

The second stage involved samples of families drawn from those known to the Siblings Support Group. In total over 100 children and young people attended the support group (lasting up to eight weeks for a block session). At the start of the research the children's centre which ran the groups provided 60 family names from which completed questionnaires might be expected. Out of the 60 questionnaires sent out, some 41 were returned; a 68 per cent response rate. Family interviews were arranged with a sample of 18 families, who agreed (on the questionnaire) that their non-disabled child could participate in a one-to-one interview with one of us. I also asked the child, at interview, whether they agreed to being interviewed – all did.

In the third stage of the research a further 15 questionnaires were received from families whose children did not attend a siblings support group. The intention was to provide data which could be compared with that received from families whose children did attend a support group. The siblings group may be referred to as the 'experimental' group, while the group not experiencing the benefits of sibling-group activity becomes the control group (Corbetta 2003, p.97). If differences are found between the two groups, these may be attributed to the sibling-group attendance effect. A control group enables the reliability of the data to be evaluated, so that differences occurring in one group do not occur in another, and the intervening variable, in this case the effect of the sibling group, can be shown to make a difference to the experience of the siblings involved. The control group without a sibling-group influence enabled the sibling-group data to be compared, to ascertain whether the sibling-group membership predisposed those involved toward a particular response bias. The control group reported an equal enthusiasm for sibling-group attendance as found among sibling-group members, demonstrating a recognition that some form of additional service input is required.

Finally, two group meetings were held for siblings at the children's centre following a suggestion by the advisory group. This was thought necessary to clarify whether any siblings felt constrained by their home environment, reflected by the expression of different views when not at home: the group interviews would demonstrate whether the responses from the home interviews were consistently reflected in the group discussion: this is a test-retest technique (Corbetta 2003, p.81) and is necessary to ensure that data are reliable. The intent is to ensure that data are not contaminated by a family view, which might be expected to influence the sibling in the home environment, but should not do so away from home when the 'family constraint' is removed. Two groups of siblings were led by an adult older sibling with a disabled brother or sister, who encouraged discussion in two groups (each of eight) on the experience of living with a disabled sibling. The group facilitators were provided with a copy of Appendix 2 to enable some consistency with the questions asked; the facilitators recorded comments, and transcripts were used to inform the database of case material retained for the study.

Data analysis

The questionnaire was designed for variable analysis using SPSS Release 4.0 on a Macintosh PC. In all 74 variables were identified and coded for the production of frequency tables and cross-tabulations, mainly to produce bivariate data, with partial tables to reflect differing groups. A coded number was entered on the questionnaire, to the right of each question, to show individual responses (Appendix 1). When nominal variables are reduced to two categories they can be treated, in a statistical sense, as higher order variables (Corbetta 2003 p.71). Using bivariate data (i.e. in a 2 x 2 table) meant the non-linear or ordinal data could be treated as having an interval or ratio relationships. Essentially, categories of relationships are non-linear, but division into higher and lower orders enables comparisons to be made which can then be tested for levels of significance which increases confidence in the results in terms of their applicability to the general population (Williams 2003, p.139).

Establishing 'face validity'

Bivariate tables help in the formulation of typologies, the construction of which is part of problem-solving techniques, when information which may be of normative origin and lacks empirical vigour has to be translated into a suitable form for analysis (Pearlman 1957, pp.53–58). However, this difficulty in representing the situation of siblings is overcome by reducing group data into a bivariate form under which associations may be examined. The difficulty lies in grouping the various categories into appropriate bivariate forms. Glazer (1965) in a quote by Smith (1975) coded each incident in as many categories as possible to enable a constant comparative method. This brings into play the skills of the social researcher to devise a means for reducing the data into its bivariate form, the success of which will have an immediate 'face validity' when associations are reported which assist in explaining the phenomenon being examined. 'Face validity' is referred to by Moser and Kalton (1971, p.355) the resultant scale that measures attitudes, in this case the data succeeds by the fact of its immediate relevance to the groups concerned (see Tables 4.1, 4.2 and 4.3 in Chapter 4). The method of data compression followed is subjective to a degree, but benefits by enabling higher-order analysis to take place, which aids data interpretation.

Further research

Despite efforts to ensure data reliability, utilising a pilot study which included a control group, the study cited is relatively small in scale, and results, even when significant, only provide an evaluation of the population examined. These results need to be treated with a little caution, therefore, even though the impact of disability on siblings is reported with some confidence. As with most research reported, some wider-scale repetition would increase the reliability of the findings, which, nevertheless, emerge consistently during the work reported here to inform the situation of siblings with disabled brothers and sisters.

Chapter 3

The Impact of Disability on the Family

In this chapter I will start by examining the difference that having a new baby with disabilities may make to the family, at birth and subsequently and particularly with reference to brothers and sisters. In my research, when I write about the family I usually mean the biological family and mention parents as the carers of their disabled child, because parents were predominantly the primary carers who responded to the research questionnaires in two different studies (Burke and Cigno 1996, Burke and Montgomery 2001b). The term 'carer' is used here to mean parents, although it could mean carers who are not the child's parents; but parents and carers are used synonymously within this text. Siblings within the family may also be involved in caring responsibilities, looking after their disabled brother or sister, and consequently the role of siblings as carers is also discussed but separately from that of parents as the primary or main carers.

The obvious place to start a chapter on the impact of child disability on the family is with the birth of the disabled child, and although the label of disability may or may not be applicable, the sense of difference, for siblings, in having a new brother or sister will have begun.

A new child

The birth of any baby will have an impact on the lives of all the family, which includes siblings. The new baby will make demands that have to be met above all by his or her parents or carers. At the very least, a new baby is an extra focus of interest for all family members, but a new baby in the family is also a source of potential stress, because the family is experiencing the effects of a major change to its constitution (Busfield 1987).

The initial feature of having a new baby in the family is usually one which celebrates the arrival of the new child. Having a new child also requires major family readjustments whether or not any suspicion of disability may have risen. However, some parents will be informed, prior to birth, that the new baby will be disabled. Indeed, with the advent of antenatal testing, a baby's future disability can be determined, and whether to continue with the pregnancy could even have been an issue for the parents.

In this text the question of the right of the unborn child to birth is upheld, but the issue of whether medical interventions, such as, for example, amniocentesis (using a needle to examine for abnormalities within the amniotic fluid during the early stages of pregnancy) or other diagnostic techniques is required because screening may determine whether the prospect of a termination of an otherwise healthy but possibly disabled child is 'carried-out'. It remains a difficult situation to discuss and examine without all the facts pertaining to the family and the unborn child. However, such matters will be faced by some families and will have consequences for the acceptance or otherwise of the disabled child, not only at birth, but also throughout the child's development (see Burke and Cigno 2000, p.87).

A child with disabilities will not only be different in various ways, but will certainly require even more attention from those charged with his or her care (Moeller 1986). The identification of 'special needs', as it might be put, will often occur following the identification of disability, whether prior to birth, at birth or at some later stage of the child's early years. In my research (Burke and Montgomery 2001b) nearly 50 per cent of infants had their disability confirmed before they were 1 year old. There then seems to be a slowing-off of diagnosis. By the time the children in the sample (n =

59) were 5 years old, nearly 84 per cent of them had a confirmed diagnosis. The reporting of a child's disability at birth has a different impact on the family from one diagnosed at the age of 5: the children are at different stages developmentally and parental reactions will not be the same.

On being told that your child is disabled or different

The impact of disability may not, therefore, occur until the baby is noticed to be somehow 'different' during the stages of normal childhood development. The impact of diagnosis of disability is often a shock to parents and they are likely to experience a mixture of emotions, ranging from the delight of having a new-born child to anger, denial and grief (Frude 1991; Knight, 1996; Russell 1997). In one instance, reported to me during an interview, a parent discovered that her 18-month-old child had 'a disability' when a consultant pediatrician, who had been monitoring the child's development owing to premature birth said, 'Paul will be able to use the specialised child care provisions locally, including respite foster care.' In discussion it transpired that the services mentioned were evidently those provided for children with disabilities. The 'coded message' was that 'your child is disabled'. The parents reported that, although they did not enter into any detailed discussion with the consultant, they later questioned the meaning attributed to the initial remark in discussion together. They were attempting to ascertain whether the comment really meant that Paul had a disability or that he was in need of some form of additional help. The latter confusion was also typified in another family's experience, on being told that the child in question had 'a development delay'. In this example the child's parents interpreted the expression to mean that their child 'would catch up and progress like any other child'. They did not initially realise the underlying message that their child had some form of learning disability and that this would remain a permanent feature of the child's intellectual capacity. The issue of 'uncertainty' is one that is not uncommon when news is imparted that has some shock value because it may identify a difference that is not desired, and a sequence of adjustments has to begin, somewhat similar to those identified with loss or bereavement (Kübler-Ross 1969). The point here is, if the impact of disability is confused by coded messages, how will siblings receive the message that their brother or sister is 'disabled' or in other way different, when the child's parents may not themselves be sure? Although an expressive understanding of childhood disability, or difference, indicated by Bridge (1999, p.73), is to be found in children as young as 4 or 5, even the most perceptive sibling would find difficulty in deciphering a coded message from professionals which leaves parents without a clear understanding of their child's condition. This is not the best way to help adjustments towards an eventual acceptance (more of this will be discussed in Chapter 5 in examining 'change'), although the seeds of uncertainty may be sown early as part of an initial misunderstanding of what is meant by 'disability'.

The label 'disabled', once understood, may in itself result in negative reactions from family members and from others known to the family (Middleton 1996) who then perceive the child as somehow different from others. This is equally true for siblings who perceive some difference in their brother or sister. The confirmation of disability is nevertheless a 'shock' and clarity rather than coded messages is preferable to the uncertainty of not knowing. However, the early experience of 'difference' may not be an immediate reality, especially during the initial days when baby comes home and the level of attention from parents or carers will be similar to that of a normally developing baby. The difference is that such attention is unlikely to diminish and may increase when disabilities are severe, and will continue for as long as the child remains at home. The consequences for parents caring for a disabled child are that the additional demands leave less time and opportunity for attention for other children.

Brothers and sisters of disabled children experience a secondary form of disability – as Glendinning (1986) expressed it, siblings 'may experience the disadvantages as well' (p.3), especially when caring for a child with disabilities is charged with emotional stress through demands placed on carers. What seems likely is that when a child has disabilities, siblings will be affected in some way and, as a consequence, they will have to learn to live with their disabled brother or sister, and experiene some association with the disability itself.

Sibling rivalry

In an attempt to understand the differences between brothers and sisters, one way forward is to consider the impact of sibling rivalry. Sibling rivalry is nothing new, and Kew (1975, p.84) explained it in terms of the feelings that a child may have, including 'jealousy and resentment towards his rival brother or sister, and may entertain hostile thoughts or indulge in "aggressive behaviour"'. Within the context of disability sibling rivalry may present an additional difficulty for families that cope with situations outside the usual because sibling reactions may, typically, include adverse emotional stress (Seligman and Darling 1989). Siblings, growing up with a brother or sister as part of the family, will be less aware of the need for a diagnosis label, because this will be of little consequence for the sibling they live with and accept without needing to question such matters. Yet, even though a label may not be the most important factor in sibling relationships, the sense of difference, initially identified in the pilot study (Burke and Montgomery 2001a), became a potential source of frustration and confusion between brothers and sisters with disabled siblings. Indeed, as mentioned earlier (Bridge 1999), siblings as young as 4 or 5 were aware of differences in their siblings. This awareness appears to increase when siblings get older and are, perhaps, more curious about their brother's or sister's disability.

Siblings also share the stress experienced by their parents at the time of the birth of their disabled sibling or at the time when the realisation of disability sets in (Seligman 1991). The presence of the newborn infant can lead to resentment by siblings who may feel that their brother or sister requires and gains too much attention and disproportionate consideration (Coleman 1990). The impact on siblings of having a brother or sister with disabilities will increase the sense of being 'left out' which often goes unrecognised within the family and requires a degree of family refocusing to correct. Professional help would be potentially valuable at such times even though families may not immediately accept that their situation requires some form of intervention.

Like parents, brothers and sisters need information about disability, a need which will change over time with their understanding, and in line with the differences in the developmental stages achieved by the disabled child in the family.

The impact of disability during a child's cognitive development

According to Lobato (1990) preschool children, for instance, need simple 'concrete' explanations suitable for their developmental level. Kew (1975) found that parents' ability to cope with a disabled child was one of the factors affecting the welfare of siblings. A readjustment to the new situation is necessary, balancing the competing demands of living with a new baby, which Powell and Ogle (1985) recognise as affecting both the structure of the newly constituted family and its functional ability to manage.

It is important, therefore, to understand how siblings cope with the change in their status and standing compared with children in non-disabled families, and whether the consequences of any additional burdens placed upon them are redressed in other ways. As I mentioned earlier, while most parents believe that their children might be affected by living with a disabled sibling, this does not necessarily mean that the experience works in an adverse way. Children with disabilities are children and will react as children, and each bring their own share of uplifting as well as difficult experiences.

Watson (1991) reflects on the positive experience siblings will gain from living with a disabled sibling, thanks to the insight gained into caring relationships which extend somewhat beyond the norm for most families. In the work of Lobato (1990) and in the earlier work of Blackard and Barsch (1982) there is evidence that relationships within families were strengthened when caring for a child with disabilities. Such a finding is somewhat in conflict with others: Frude (1991), for example, discusses the differences experienced, suggesting that some families experience caring for a disabled child as a crisis, even though others become more united, working together to overcome difficulties. People do not have stereotypical response and consequently needs will not be the same in all families.

Siblings of children with disabilities develop special qualities and, while all children have the capacity to respond to and care for others, the way in which they do so reflects their own individual differences. These need time to be understood, for the vulnerability of childhood is such that misunderstanding may provoke a lifetime of uncertainty. Weighing up the available evidence, it is possible to conclude that in most cases the daily challenges of caring will be perceived as greater by parents; and siblings are in danger of not always having normal childhood expectations met. Indeed, depending on the nature of a child's disability, some children may witness their brother or sister suffer serious illness, with the prospect that they may die (Weatherup 1991).

As siblings grow up and ponder their future role as brothers and sisters, they may increasingly feel that they face, and share, many of the challenges experienced by their parents (Mayer and Vadasy 1997). Mayhew and Munn (1995) found that when siblings take on a caring role they form an unspoken alliance with their parents, which gave them a higher 'status' within the family; that does not equip them for the uncertainty of the adult world, however, and excessive responsibility will induce stress within the individual.

The case of Jane and Richard (high negative reaction)

Jane, aged 7, and Richard, her 5-year-old brother with profound disabilities, live with both parents in a comfortable terraced house within a major residential area of a Northern city. Jane's mother describes herself as a full-time carer. Her partner, James, a furniture maker, is in full-time employment, often working 12-hour shifts.

Richard has multiple disabilities including mobility difficulties, verbal dyspraxia, hearing impairment, incontinence and a heart condition. He has normal intelligence despite his problems and attends mainstream school. The latter has a special purpose-built medical room where he is assisted by two carers when requiring physical exercises or rest periods. His mobility is awkward and he needs a wheelchair if he is not to tire excessively after walking short distances.

Jane's experience of associated disability

Jane first experienced difficulties at school after Richard moved to her school approximately a year prior to interview. Previously she had performed well in class and was attentive to Richard at home, but now, according to mother, is thought to be borderline special needs. Jane's life experience is considered by the family to be abnormal, exemplified by the fact that she spent a year living with her nana following Richard's birth, a period during which he required extensive surgery. Some two years later Jane was visiting, in rotation, three different hospitals, because of family illnesses, including a period involving operative procedures performed on Richard. Her grandfather, for whom she had a special attachment, died about this time, after a period in hospital.

Jane has experienced Richard's need for special attention as a source of frustration. She has watched her brother receive special attention and seems to understand that he has overcome major life-threatening difficulties. At one time she joined her brother on a holiday, funded by a charity that provided holidays for children with disabilities, and was aware that it was her brother's holiday, although she enjoyed herself. Now that Richard is attending her school, and has special needs and attendants, it appears to have increased her sense of everything centring on Richard's needs and not her own. As reported by Burke and Montgomery (2001b) Mother describes Richard's early experience at Jane's school as follows: 'At school he had his own entourage – two school helpers and a nursing assistant. Not only staff-help, because when he started all the kids would follow him around – he was special you see.' Jane's feelings now give rise to anger, which are mainly directed at Mother, whom she will hit and verbally express her hatred of her. Her behaviour will sometimes switch and she will cry and chant prayers learnt at school, reflecting on her plight. She has kicked Richard in the stomach, knowing his sensitivity in the area, and defaced certificates he has received for his various achievements.

Comment

Generally, Jane's life experience puts her behind Richard and other family members in the queue for attention. Richard's constant need for nursing care combined with the attention any 5-year-old, younger sibling, might expect, plus the effects of a catalogue of illness within the family and extended family, must have diverted much attention from Jane, so that she now needs to be recognised as a young person with her own needs. Her high-level negative reactive (see Figure 2.1 (1)) is as an intelligent 7-year-old coping with the stress of partial exclusion, for it will seem to her that her own needs have taken second, even third place, to her brother's and other family members'. However, despite her own uncertainties, Jane will fetch and carry for mum when asked to do so but as mother reports, this often requires shouting and occasional threats to ensure that she does as requested.

Interestingly, when Jane does receive one-to-one attention, for example, when staying on her own at her maternal grandmother's, and her behaviour improves, as it does when attending a group or therapy session, and it seems that Jane craves the attention usually available in families where the attention needs of all siblings is to some extent more equally divided.

The following case example demonstrates how siblings will experience differing reactions to a younger brother, Harry, who is severely disabled and the youngest in the family. The brother nearer in age to Harry experiences a stronger behavioural reaction than his two elder brothers.

The case of Harry and brothers (mixed reactions)

Harry (aged 5 years) lives with his mother, a lone parent, and three older brothers, John, aged 15, James, aged 13 and Douglas, aged 10. Harry was born with microcephaly, and suffers from epilepsy. The latter is controlled by a twice-daily administration of prescribed drugs. Mother describes Douglas as being like a 6-month-old baby who is happy and sociable. The home is a comfortable terraced house with four bedrooms situated within a market town. Family life tends to be restrictive because Harry's disabilities means that outings for the whole family are difficult to arrange. This trouble persists despite the ownership of a 'people carrier', the family car, because of the practical problems of loading and unloading Harry's wheelchair, and difficulty parking, despite using a disabled person's car badge.

Life for the family is in other ways relatively conventional. Harry attends a special school and mother feels that she is totally committed to her four sons. However, her expressed sentiment that, once her children started infant school, the school should teach them how to manage independently, does not square with Harry's needs.

The older children are encouraged to be independent, probably thanks to mother's view that once they attend school children should become independent. Harry represents something of a paradox because he is very dependent at home where he is put in a playpen and treated like a baby, separating him from his 'independent' siblings, but he also attends school, and should, according to mother, be more independent.

Douglas and Harry (high negative reaction)

Douglas is closest in age to Harry and is the only brother in the family who has direct experience of having a brother with disabilities for most of his life, the older two seeming to 'go their own way, treating the house as a lodging place'. It may be that older siblings in this case are experiencing a not uncommon adolescent stage of development, during which uncertainty is typical (Sutton 1994). Douglas, by contrast, owing to the closer proximity of age, is more involved with his younger brother. He, like Jane, mentioned earlier, tends to fit the negative reactive category a little better. He, like Jane, has problems at school with attention difficulties and is considered something of a bully towards other schoolchildren, such a reaction possibly caused by a degree of confusion within his self-identity (Meadows 1992, p.202).

John, James and Harry (low negative reaction)

The actions of Harry's brothers seem to typify a low involvement and hence a low level of reaction to their brother. In other words, Harry's elder brothers more or less leave him to his own devices, to be cared for by his mother. John and James lead almost separate lives from that of their disabled brother, seemingly to ignore his existence – indeed, this is a form of denial since their involvement with him is minimal (see Figure 2.1(2)).

Comment

Neglectful behaviour seems to be a form of adjustment to the fact that life with disabled siblings is potentially different from that of other families.

This is simply related to the fact that the experience of living with a disabled brother is not within the usual expectations of the older brother, or indeed of most children: consequently, adjustments have to be made to enable survival within everyday social and family life. Such reactions are not necessarily a complete denial of the other's existence, (how could it be living within the same family home?), but is at least a form of remoteness or a minimisation of the impact of the other (see Hopson 1981) and in the case of John and James, Harry is still a 'baby' in the family, especially so given his high dependency needs. In the case of Douglas the closer proximity of age appears to lead to anger, as within the bereavement process mentioned earlier, and is about the physical loss of a sibling like those other children encountered in everyday experiences. In Douglas' case, his anger is channelled into bullying behaviour in the school playground.

The case of Harry and his brothers has another important feature; they live in a single-parent household. The Family Fund Trust (http://www.jrforg.uk/knowledge/findings/socialcarer, 2003) reports that families with disabled children are more likely to be single-parent families, due, in part, to the strain put on marriages, especially where two or more children have disabilities. Indeed, recognition of the undervalued status of single mothers who carry on meeting their children's needs after partners have succumbed to the strain of family life was a factor examined by Cigno and Burke (1997) when considering the support needs of the family.

Family stress

The impact of stress is associated with difficult experiences at home and at school and might lead to expressions of regret concerning disabled siblings. This was a not uncommon reaction, as I found in my research (Burke and Montgomery 2003), where regret may be expressed as 'making life too hard or difficult' compared with perceptions of the lives led by non-disabled families. The above views, however, are seemingly inconsistent with findings (Burke and Montgomery 2003) concerning the consequences of disability on the family. Nearly three-quarters of families (31 out of 42) reported that they found it difficult to do things together and had 'less time for brothers and sisters' owing to the needs of their disabled child; consequently, siblings experience some loss of attention.

In terms of inclusion, then, it may seem to be the case that difference, however perceived, affects the self-concept, and causes reactions within the individual concerned. The remedy is not necessarily at an individual level, for a social model of disability would indicate that perceptions of difference reflect attitudinal constraints exerted by the wider society. Acceptance at a societal level should therefore remedy some, if not all, of the difficulties encountered by siblings experiencing problems with their own self-identity. Acceptance at an individual level requires contact and association with one's sibling but, it is to be hoped, not with the experience reported on in Jane's case, which resulted in an emulation of disability. These are difficult balances to be made, and the examples cited represent some extreme cases, not conforming to the norm in terms of childhood disability, but helping towards an understanding of how disabilities and differences might be perceived by children.

Chapter 4

Family and Sibling Support

It is probably an accepted fact, even without recourse to the research, that children with disabilities require more help and support than other children. The evidence for such a proposition is there, and is to be found in the research on the subject: in work, for example, by McCormack (1978), Glendenning (1986), Burke and Cigno (1996), Burke and Montgomery (2001a, b). It is not my intention to debate such a settled argument but to raise concern about the brothers and sisters of children with disabilities. Indeed, according to Atkinson and Crawford (1995) approximately 80 per cent of children with disabilities have non-disabled siblings and, while the need for shared parental care will be a matter of concern for all families, the impact of living with a disabled child will challenge the available 'share of care' available from parents to a greater or lesser degree.

One question which a parent might ask (and there will be many) is 'What difference does giving more time to a disabled child than siblings make to the family?' Asking such a question is basic to my research interests and by examining family relationships and caring arrangements some answers will be found. It is with such an examination in mind that this chapter was written.

The basics are simple: if one child needs more attention than another, less time is available for the other and doing things together may not be possible. Parents are aware that siblings may suffer from a lack of attention: according to an OPCS survey (Bone and Meltzer 1989) 48 per cent of parents thought that they had less time for other siblings. The Department of Health and Social Welfare (1986) showed that when a child had several disabilities, 72 per cent of parents thought that siblings were affected to some extent. It appears that the time available to the non-disabled child is in an inverse ratio to the needs of the disabled child: the greater the needs of the child with a disability, the greater the reduction in the time available to the parent in caring for siblings.

The impact of childhood disability on the family must therefore be profound but, again, this will vary according to the type of disability and how it manifests itself. Additional variables will concern the families themselves, since all will not respond to the needs of their children in exactly the same way. Yet, as I shall show, siblings who are denied their share of attention will, nevertheless, be a major help to their parents in sharing caring responsibilities. Others may not agree: for example, Beresford (1994) found that brother and sisters did not have to undertake special or unusual tasks to help their disabled sibling, a finding apparently confirmed by Connors and Stalker (2003) because siblings did not have a significant role in helping their disabled brother or sister.

Although some researchers indicate that brothers and sisters are not usually relied on for practical support, a considerable number of writers and researchers (for example, Glendinning 1986) suggest that many children are adversely affected by the presence of a sibling with disabilities. They may, for example, 'miss out' on certain events and activities because the family is unable to participate because of competing pressures (Sone 1993). Adolescents may find it difficult to bring friends home. Sibling relationships may be strained, especially where one child has severe learning difficulties (Philip and Duckworth 1982) or when disability is associated with behaviour problems (Powell and Ogle 1985).

My research on siblings was based on a population of 56 families with 177 children (Burke and Montgomery 2003) and would indicate that siblings have a helping role within the family, particularly if accepting the siblings' view (119 in the survey: see Chapter 2, Part 2 for a more detailed discussion on methodology), which, as I will show, is not necessarily in agreement with that of their parents. However, it must be said, the evidence is not conclusive, and it is perhaps more indicative than an accepted fact, but it appears that siblings do help out more than parents probably realise, even though the question concerning the 'nature of help' offered may only be defined intuitively by the children themselves. My findings would therefore agree with those of Glendinning (1986), McHale and Gamble (1987), and Sone (1993) who generally found that siblings had a caring role for their disabled sibling within the family. Clearly, the relationship between a child with disabilities and its siblings is not necessarily on exactly the same footing as that which exists when neither sibling is disabled, although it may be expected that younger children look to older siblings for child-related and other activities (Meadows 1992, p.188). For example, older siblings assume an adult role to help educate their younger siblings (Dunn and Kendrick 1982).

The presence of a disabled child may bring new opportunities and understanding to other family members, although, generally, this may mean that the needs of brothers and sisters receive less attention. Such differences are found to some degree in any family but risks may be greater in families with a disabled child, especially when the child concerned has difficulty in articulating their needs, or cannot express matters as clearly as their siblings, relatives or friends.

Quality Protects, Sure Start and ethnic groups

The focus of this book is on the particular needs of siblings who have different experiences from those of children without a disabled brother or sister. Siblings also require some attention if professionals are to help the whole family. The Department of Health (1991) in its Guidance and Regulations, clearly recognises this need, stating that siblings' needs 'should be provided for as part of a package of services for the child with a disability' (sec. 6.4, p.13). The Department of Health (1998) *Quality Protects* initiative is designed to help families and children with disabilities to gain priority consideration, although the situation concerning siblings remain enmeshed in 'children in need' and is not specifically identified. Government-funded programmes like 'Sure Start' are established for families who experience social exclusion and will help improve the lot of children in disadvantaged areas; 'Sure Start' has been well received, but has a limited focus on the needs of disabled children and their siblings (Sure Start web page, http://www.surestart.gov.uk/news, 2003). The exception, from three listed, is one which has set up a multi-agency partnership for families with disabled children in Bournemouth, provides support to families, and may even award small grants. However, at the time of writing no project exists concerning the needs of siblings of children with disabilities.

Within the *Quality Protects* work programme (http://www.doh. gov.uk/qualityprotects/work_pro/project/work) to incorporate the needs of Black and ethnic minority children is a key objective, and in many ways siblings and disabled children and minority groups are similarly disadvantaged, although siblings and disabled children who are also Black and from ethnic minority groups, as identified by Phillips (1998), must experience a double disadvantage, as the following case clearly demonstrates.

The case of Rani and Ahmed (high negative reaction)

Rani is a 12-year-old girl who attends a special school, as does her brother, Ahmed, who is 9. Both children live at home with their mother and father. Ahmed is diagnosed with attention deficit hyperactivity disorder (ADHD) and would tend to violent activity at home, although the family report some success with prescribed medication, one consequence being a weight gain and only moderate control over his behaviour. He would attack his sister for no apparent reason and needed constant supervision to maintain any semblance of peace in the home.

Rani has started at a local mainstream school at the age of 5, but experienced what her parents described as 'a total ignoring' by other children. Mother said that as a family they wished to be integrated within the community but after 15 years had little success in their local village community. They put this down to living in a village where there were no other people from similar backgrounds to themselves (Muslim, Asian). The fact that Ahmed has behavioural problems marked the family as even more different from others' and Rani, whom the family consider is perfectly normal, has had to go to a special school, in their view, due to the stress experienced within the local mainstream one: 'she could not make any friends'. Rani eventually received a statement of special educational needs (Department of Education and Skills 2001) and is performing only moderately well within the special school, which the family feels is the only option open to her.

The family express the view that they have been discriminated against because of their race and culture. This has been exacerbated by their son's disability, and the combination of the two has effectively disabled their daughter, Rani, purely as the result of the oppressive reactions of other people. The family (actually the parents) say that they feel bitter, angry and totally ostracised by their local community. The only help available is an enlightened support group provided by the local Independent Education Advisory Service, which caters for children and families in the area. It has offered help to both Ahmed and Rani and generated a feeling of acceptance from other children who attend; the group has also helped both parents.

Comment

This is probably the most extreme case encountered during my research: the case stems from the control family which did not have an available sibling support group, and points out the totally unacceptable behaviour that community life may provoke. The lifeline to this family is slender, but the IEAS is providing a helpful support group for the whole family, although the damage to Rani and Ahmed cannot be calculated. The case demonstrated a highly negative reactive experience, but this is not due to disability alone: in part, it is based on perceived community hostility. Disability by association is clearly Rani's experience, if it can be quantified in that way, but the double disability is due to racist intolerance for a family doing its best to manage. The controlled dignity shown in the interview leaves one full of amazement at the tolerance of the family on one side and the intolerance of others on the other.

Group support

Help for siblings is, nevertheless, available at a practical level as Tozer (1996) found when siblings were introduced to groups formed for siblings themselves, and within the protective setting of the group they could express their feelings. This is exactly the situation confirmed by my own research (Burke and Montgomery 2003), when a specially formed siblings support group provided a youth-club type environment for children with 'disabled siblings' where they could engage in activities or simply discuss matters within a stigma-free setting. The support Rani and Ahmed found was not within a siblings group, but in another context, demonstrating the power of group forces in raising the self-esteem of individual members.

The question of support for Black and minority ethnic families was examined by Chamba *et al.* (1999), who showed that Black families were more likely to receive support from their own families than white families were, but that service provision discriminates against Black families and their communities. Service provision clearly needs to take account of cultural, linguist and religious needs; unfortunately this does not necessarily follow, whichever culture one belongs to, as I shall demonstrate.

In order to understand the situation of brothers and sisters, it is useful to distinguish between the special needs of a child with disabilities and those of a brother or sister. I shall illustrate how these differences affect their lives and draw on the evidence available from case examples to show how professional attention and an assessment might identify brothers' and sisters' needs and point to ways in which they might be met.

Indeed, disability by association, shows that the emotional needs of children with disabilities and their siblings may not be that different, especially for siblings with high negative reactions (Table 2.1: Chapter 2) who come to emulate some aspects of disability themselves. In such circumstances support workers may effectively be assisting a family with two disabled children, which would add to the 17,000 families with two or more disabled children identified by Tozer (1999). If we consider the additive effect of disability by association, from the 22 families interviewed, there were four siblings in this category, approximately one in five. However, it is impossible to generalise such a trend to families with siblings of disabled children, although the impact is clear enough within the families interviewed.

In Table 4.1 I show the views of parents as expressed within a questionnaire concerning their disabled children and whether they consider that siblings share in their caring responsibilities. The results are reported in more detail in Burke and Montgomery (2003) but I shall recap here to

Table 4.1: Parental views of the benefits of having a disabled child compared with their perceptions of siblings' caring responsibilities

(adapted from Burke and Montgomery 2003)

		Siblings help with caring		
		yes	no	row total (%)
Benefits in having a disabled child	some	37	3	40 (71.4)
	none	9	7	16 (28.6)
column total (%)		46 (82.1)	10 (17.9)	56 (100.0)

Chi-Square: 10.24, DF: 1, Significance greater than .002

illustrate the fact that siblings helped care for their disabled brother or sister. Over 80 per cent of parents (46) reported that their non-disabled child helped with the caring responsibilities (including play-type activities, see Chapter 5) of looking after their disabled brother or sister, and over 70 per cent (40) indicated that that having a disabled child brought positive benefits to the family. Most parents clearly recognised that caring for a child with disabilities had both positive and negative elements and that siblings were helpful with some caring tasks. However, not all shared this view, some 12 per cent (7) of parents indicating that there were no benefit in having a disabled child, and these same parents indicated that they considered that their non-disabled children did not help with caring responsibilities. Perhaps it is no surprise that parents who had negative views about their disabled child also had negative views about their siblings. When such views prevail, it seems that siblings are not recognised as offering any help or caring within the family by their parents – such a situation seems almost inconceivable given any rational understanding of family dynamics, and the reality is often that siblings do help with caring activities but their input goes unrecognised. The results for Table 4.1 are significant in a statistical sense and, in order to understand this situation, we need also to understand why family attitudes are as they are and to find out why the differences in attitude seemingly discriminate against siblings in the family. Indeed, it may be because the process of adjustment to disability is something parents have to accommodate (see Chapter 5) that some distortion of perception results and sibling's help is not acknowledged.

The question then is 'how do negative attitudes affect siblings?' If parents do not recognise the input of siblings, what hope is there for anyone else to understand their situation? Clearly experiences away from home, as a family with a disabled child, are not focused on the needs of siblings, and are unlikely to promote insight into the needs of siblings. It is necessary for an enlightened professionals to begin to realise that some form of support is needed when little is forthcoming within the home. It should be clear that the numbers mentioned in Table 4.1 are low, and despite their significance, all siblings may not be suffering a lack of recognition by parents. However, when it does occur, it will promote a secondary sense of disability, compounding the situation of disability existing within the family by the exclusion of siblings' needs.

In Table 4.2 I have reproduced data from my earlier research (Burke and Cigno 1996) because this provides some insight into parental contact with professional services. Basically 9 parents out of 67 had low contact with informal networks (family, friends or neighbours) and with professionals (school, health or welfare) when low equated with less than monthly for informal contacts and less than three monthly for professional

Table 4.2: Family contact with formal and informal social networks				
(adapted from Burke and Cigno 1996, p.67)				
		professional network		
		low	high	row total (%)
Informal network	low	9	16	25 (37.3)
	high	2	40	42 (62.7)
column total (%)		11 (16.4)	56 (83.6)	67 (100)
Chi-Square: 11.14, DF: 1, Significance greater than .001				

contacts. Notably, the majority of families (40) had good networks of support, but again, like attitudes towards siblings, it is the low-contact family that caused concern. If a low-contact family is also a negative perceiver of sibling help, it seems probable that the situation of siblings is likely to be increasingly fraught. This is speculative, for it may not be the case that low contact and negative perception co-exist or are indeed associated situations other than in this study. The issues remain, nevertheless, since whatever reasons low contact, or isolation and negative perceptions continue, they will impact on siblings, and this is an indicator of the need for professional involvement.

In order to understand the need for contact with professionals as part of my research (Burke and Montgomery 2003) a response to questions within a survey questionnaire revealed that 10 out of 41 families with children attending a siblings support group (significance better than .05%) indicated that they had low contact with professional workers and were low users of services (see Table 4.3).

Table 4.3: Professional involvement and service provision (for sibling group)

(adapted from Burke and Montgomery 2003)

		services provided		
		yes	no	row total (%)
Professional support usually available	yes	17	5	22 (53.7)
	no	9	10	19 (46.3)
column total (%)		26 (63.4)	15 (36.6)	41 (100)
Chi-Squares: 3.9, DF: 1, Significance greater than .05				

A higher rate of services used was associated (for 17 families) with higher levels of contact between professional workers and the family of the child attending the support group. It appears simply to be the case that families that keep in regular touch with professionals (defined by more than three-monthly contacts) receive more help in the form of service provision and, whether by design or omission, the professional neglect or exclusion of involvement of users reduces the demand on services. To express this simply, if families do not seek services they will not receive them, and it appears families with the most needs may be reluctant to ask for assistance. Clearly a proactive role for professional support is indicated particularly for such families, as indicated in Tables 4.1 and 4.2 where negative attitudes and low levels of interpersonal contact exist. However, it must be said, that inclusion of the data from the control group (15 families) dispersed the association found in Table 4.3, which might suggest that attendance at the sibling group tended to improve the provision of services. This might be expected, where services are more finely tuned, albeit still revealing a worrying number of families not receiving the same degree of service input.

I would suggest that professional involvement is necessary for otherwise 'at-risk' families. 'At-risk' is defined here as relative isolation, or low involvement and participation within their community. In these circumstances siblings cannot fare well, and even in the responses received, part of that risk was potentially reduced by attendance at a siblings group, so that the levels of unmet need are likely to be even greater than my own research suggests, for those siblings who did not attend the support group and for those families in isolation that failed to respond to the invitation to participate in the research. Such views are speculative, but the trend seems clear and professionals need to reach out to those most in need, and any 'don't ask, don't get' philosophy should be abhorred.

The need for support and counselling for siblings as young carers is also stressed by Thompson (1995). Thompson discusses the intense feelings of siblings in their familial relationships as involving rivalry and jealousy (of the child with a disability because of the perceived attention he or she receives) and indicates how important it is for parents to set limits for each of their children, to make consequences for actions age-appropriate and fair and to make sure that each child receives parental attention. Lee and de Majo (1994) make a similar point, adding that siblings may be at risk of displaced anger from parents, and to prevent this, parents and their children need support.

In the following case example, drawn for my research interview, Daniel has different experiences from his older siblings, suggesting that a closer age proximity has a bearing on the impact of disability on the sibling. The experience of Daniel fits within a compliant form of reaction to disability.

The case of Daniel and brothers Joe and David (compliant behaviour)

Daniel, aged 10, is diagnosed as autistic. He lives with his parents and his brother, Joe, aged 14, and David, aged 18 months. The family home is a three-story town house on the outskirts of a Northern city.

Mother says that she suspected that Daniel was 'different' immediately following his birth; he was always crying as a baby, would not communicate like other infants and did not respond to stimulation in the same way that his older brother had. Autism was not confirmed until Daniel was 6 years old. He now attends a special school for children with autism.

According to Mother, Daniel tends to be hyperactive at home and this can include being violent towards his older brother, although at school he seems to be better behaved. Daniel's father is able to control him by physical restraint without harming him, but Daniel has caused actual harm to his younger 'baby' brother, David, because he does not realise the consequences of certain of his actions. On one occasion Daniel pushed David so hard that David cut his hand badly as he fell to the ground. Despite such upsets, the children seem well, and problems that do occur are more often a result of rather extreme behaviour at the end of 'rough and tumble' play, than any deliberate malice. Unfortunately, Daniel is not very aware of the consequences of his actions but will, however, play on the 'Playstation' games consul for hours on end.

Joe and Daniel

Joe told me that he got into fights with Daniel, but more often this involved 'fighting-back, as needed' because Daniel would attack him and as he himself would not strike Daniel or initiate an attack, it was merely 'self-defence'. Joe had learned to tolerate his brother rather than to get on well with him because he had no choice in the matter.

Joe told me that he enjoyed attending a siblings group, but freely admitted that he had not kept in contact with any of the other young people that he had met. He said he liked meeting people and the activities that were followed, although he could not say what actually happened when he went to the group sessions.

David: A child protection issue

David was too young to engage in any discussion, but the nature of the family relationships suggested that he could be at risk in the presence of Daniel if left unsupervised. Indeed, Daniel's needs are complex and his behaviour hard to predict. There are clearly child protection issues here, which need professional assessment, especially within a family that is not entirely competent in the management of its own affairs, and lacking the ability to express their need clearly. Preventing the exposure to risk is a social-work responsibility and a duty under the Children Act 1989, Section 47, where an assessment of the family situation will indicate the need for further intervention. The family seems vulnerable to me and would benefit from the more direct involvement of a social worker, to monitor needs and to explore areas of assistance which might be provided. As matters stand, a social worker is involved with the family, although the role, as expressed to me, is linked mainly to Joe's attendance at the sibling group.

Comment

Fighting seemed to be an acceptable family trait, in a family where communication on a verbal level seemed difficult, or at least it appeared so in my interview and, although there may have been an interviewer effect, other clues were suggestive of a household with low verbal expectations. The focus on the physical seemed reflected by a large weight-training bench in the middle of the living room, with varying weights surrounding the bench, ready it seemed, for immediate use. Mention was made of a relative who was thought to be autistic, in the sense of not speaking, and overall the family seemed reluctant to discuss matters, despite responding positively by asking a friend to help fill in and return the survey questionnaire. It appeared that filling in a form was a difficult task, yet the willingness to help was clearly there. Perhaps the meeting was viewed as an official exchange rather than one in which information could be freely discussed: the willingness to be available was not matched by an easy exchange in discussion. The family seemed self-sufficient and unused to seeking help from others, preferring instead to go it alone, as is their right, but one worries that the consequences of under-stimulation, if this is a correct assessment, could adversely impact on all the siblings in the family. Indeed, during interview, late in the evening, the room was dimly lit, and it was difficult to read notes and engage in any eye contact, further restricting the level of communication achieved.

The view that Joe has a compliant reaction to disability is based simply on the fact that he believed himself to be a defender rather than an attacker regarding Daniel, who is treated in an accommodating way, tolerated and accepted within the family at the cost of outside contacts. Joe has no friends through choice and this would seem a way of managing his position within the family. Joe's role within the family is not recognised by his parents (see Table 4.1 on parental views, and Petr and Barney 1993) in any verbal expression of his abilities and the family appears to exist in some degree of isolation from professional support (see Table 4.2).

The acceptance of my own visit may indicate some need for support, within a family that might find it difficult to articulate the fact that they would welcome advice and help, if available, but in the absence of such help, would be tolerant and get on with their lives. However, 'help' in terms of professional advice never seemed far away, although the family appears reluctant to actively seek it. This may be what Marris (1974) refers to as the 'conservative impulse', when situations are treated with a degree of ambivalence and uncertainty. In Joe's case he reflects just such a family attitude, but his acceptance is more accurately described as 'compliance', because he is following what appears to be a family-induced form of reaction to events within and external to their functioning. He is mirroring a learnt response that confers the least resistance.

Finding time for family members

It is not an easy matter for parents to find sufficient time for all family members especially when one member requires special care. Such situations may lead to emotional neglect, which is possible in Joe's situation, mentioned above, and although he attended a support group for siblings this seemed not to fulfil his needs other than providing some outside activities. Possibly there is some guilt within Joe's apparent isolation from friends, failure to follow up within the support group, and apparent general apathy concerning events, but it is difficult to be sure, because his reluctance to discuss matters makes assessment difficult.

The evidence from other research supports the view that youngsters tend not to talk to others about having a disabled relative, particularly one as close as a brother or sister, or indeed about the amount of caring they may be obliged to do (Atkinson and Crawford 1995; Thompson 1995). Powell and Ogle (1985) suggest that, as well as support services, siblings need information about disabilities themselves or they may lose out on the many positive elements of childhood. What is very clear is that siblings, as well as family members, need support, to help clarify their own understanding of their needs, and professional help seems always to be accepted, despite not always appearing to be welcome or fully understood. The evidence presented here suggests that professionals need to work at gaining trust within a family, and it is not acceptable to assume that because help is not requested that it is not needed. Intervention in such circumstances requires a proactive worker, who will frequently return to the family and checking their needs for advice and service provision. Joe's family will not demand help, but they clearly need it.

Chapter 5

Children as Young Carers

It is probably an accepted fact that most families will look to themselves in times of difficulty, to resolve problems or needs that have to be met. It is probably true that siblings will always help to bring up children within the family, but the question, 'What is reasonable to expect?' is speculative and whether an expectation should extend beyond the more usually accepted norms of shared responsibility is debatable.

In this chapter the siblings of children with disabilities are considered as 'young carers'. A definition of a young carer used by the Carers National Association is:

> Anyone under the age of 18, whose life is in some way restricted because of the need to take responsibility for the care of a person who is ill, has a disability, is experiencing mental distress, is affected by substance misuse or HIV/AIDS. (identified by Rollins 2002 http://www.carersinformation.org.uk/showdoc.ihtml?id=767)

The siblings of children with disabilities may be identified as 'young carers', when they help and take responsibility for the care of a disabled brother or sister. The term 'young carers', as defined above, may also concern young people who care for a parent who is ill, has disabilities or is subject to a range of illnesses or conditions, and these are dimensions beyond siblings caring for other siblings.

Siblings are considered as young carers in recognition of the help that they offer the family in caring for a disabled brother or sister, which is considered additional to that help that may be expected or assumed within a family where the children are not considered to have a disability. This element of help in going beyond the norm is not merely an assertion, as I shall show, but is supported by empirical research evidence. The phenomenon is not only common in Britain, but is also experienced in the USA and across Europe. The degree of help offered may be considered somewhat of a subjective element, because what may seem reasonable within one family may not in another: the exceptional is due the nature and type of help offered by siblings to their disabled brother and sisters, which then enables the whole family to function that bit better.

This chapter will explore the nature of the additional and exceptional caring tasks before considering how the 'locus of control' may assist the family and professionals with assessing the support needs that arises directly from the care that is provided. I begin by considering the research on 'young carers' and the responsibilities they assume.

Research findings

Becker (2000) estimated the total numbers of family carers in Britain to be near 1 million. The number of young carers under the age of 18 years was estimated by the Loughborough University research group to be 50,000 of whom the majority were girls (Brindle 1998). Horwitz (1993) estimated that in the USA approximately one-fifth of the population do not have siblings and there the option to assist parents with the caring task is not possible, but it would seem, nevertheless, that in Britain we follow the trend in the USA, in which the majority of children with disabilities will have siblings who can offer some form of help and assistance to their parents.

Myers (1978) discusses the additional responsibility that siblings of disabled brothers and sisters accept and shows that they are expected to mature more quickly than they would if they did not have a disabled sibling. A parent encountered during my own interviews said, 'they have to grow up more quickly, don't they,' which seemed to reflect the view from two-thirds of those responding to the survey (40), indicating that siblings were more caring and aware of disabilities thanks to their home experience (Burke and Montgomery 2003). The point about 'growing-up more quickly' is repeated in the case of Fay and Michael, which is used to illustrate the experience of Fay in the final part of this chapter. Grossman (1972) reports a similar finding, cited in Powell and Ogle (1985, p.83), but express it in terms of siblings with disabled brothers or sisters who may experience pressure to take on responsibilities beyond that expected in non-disabled sibling relationship. This is learning by experience, which Allott (15.12. 2001 *Telegraph* Magazine, http://www.carersinformation. org.uk) expressed simply: 'They are children who have no time to be children'.

The fact that siblings help to care for their non-disabled children is found in evidence from research across nations. An examination by Becker (1995) concerning young carers in Britain, France, Sweden and Germany, demonstrated that young people will respond exceptionally when circumstance dictate the need to do so. In the USA Lobato (1990) and Powell and Gallagher (1993) were concerned about the needs of siblings and produced advice and guidance for parents and practitioners to help their understanding of the needs of young carers. In Britain, the Social Services Inspectorate (1996) stresses that young carers will often share responsibilities with their parents in the care offered to brothers and sisters with disabilities. In this task, nevertheless, they may feel isolated, as found by Atkinson and Crawford (1995), who indicated that an increasing sense of isolation was a common stress reaction to the combination of caring tasks which accumulated when caring for a disabled sibling, in particular, restricting the amount of time available for other activities. The need to support young carers is part of the National Carers Strategy (Department of Health 1999), although the form of that support is subject to interpretation. The Department of Health's (2000a) assessment framework may begin to clarify the needs of young carers by indicating that their needs should be addressed within the assessment undertaken by professional workers, albeit the focus is not so specifically on siblings as the 'child in need' and the family in a holistic sense, as commented on in Chapter 1.

Caring responsibilities

Becker (2000), reviewing three research studies that covered differing client groups, concluded that caring involves a 'whole family approach'. He suggests that when needs are assessed the focus should be on the whole family, and not on individuals in isolation. To achieve such an objective, researchers should understand how families experience their caring responsibilities.

My research (Burke and Montgomery 2003) supports the fact that siblings help their brothers and sisters, exceptionally where there is a disability. The nature of that help extends beyond the spectrum of help offered by others who are free from major disabilities or conditions because it is the conditions themselves which impose the additional need for caring. This is not contentious, but it is indicative of a need for increased support for those requiring additional services. A number of themes explored in my research were noted from 22 interviews with families and children. Children were interviewed separately from parents. Additionally, notes were taken at two sibling-led support group meetings, in an attempt to see whether themes identified within the original interviews were recurrent or isolated, this being a form of research triangulation to improve the reliability of the findings (see Chapter 2: Part 2, for a more detailed discussion on research methods).

In the survey questionnaire, distributed to 115 families, of the 56 replies, 82 per cent of families (45 out of 55) answered the question 'Do your non-disabled children help you with the care of their disabled brother or sister?' by replying in the affirmative. It appears then, according to parents, that the majority of siblings helped in some way with caring needs of their disabled brother or sister. According to 16 siblings interviewed, all said they helped their family with differing types of caring tasks. The nature of those responsibilities will now be explained in more detail.

Relieving the stress experienced by parents

Siblings may help by taking pressure off their parents. Tozer (1996, p.177) shows that siblings have a dual role, as carers themselves and in supporting their parents. Siegal and Silverstein (1994) also identified that when children take on a parental role they reduce the stress experienced by the main carers, usually the parents. Through being a care-giver as well as a son or daughter the child forms an alliance with their parents which, according to Mayhew and Munn (1995), gives them added status within the family.

In interview, with a girl I shall call Katy, aged 13, she recalled how she would assist her parents, by reading a story to her brother as part of his bedtime routine. Another girl, Jackie, aged 14, acknowledged that she thought it part of her responsibility to take the pressure off her parents by giving her brother her attention, thereby diverting his demands away from both parents. Chris, aged 14, would play with his sister, Mary, who had 'autistic tendencies' and would usually suffer his hair being pulled, but would not react by shouting or showing any indication of pain, having discovered that reacting encouraged more hair pulling. He never discussed this with his parents because 'they had enough to worry about'. He helped his parents by keeping his sister occupied, tolerating her behaviour in a way he would never accept from his friends and by not telling his parents about the stress Mary caused him.

The motivation to take on the role as helper may not therefore be to gain parental approval; it may be an acceptance of one's situation within the family. Seligman (1991, p.188) suggests that one explanation may be that siblings feel they must somehow compensate for the fact that they are not disabled, as my own daughter pointed out to me, as mentioned earlier, in conversations with her peers, when asked, 'Why were you the lucky one?' she would simply answer, 'I don't know', accepting by default that she is perhaps lucky not to be disabled given the fact that both her brothers have disabilities. The problem is that such encounters may well instil a sense of guilt at having similar abilities to most other children, a fact which others would never question. These examples demonstrate a form of disability by association, acceptance perhaps, from which 'young carers' would normally exclude their parents, but would 'only tell' because of 'the research interview'.

A further insight, one that helps to explain the reticence of siblings to express their opinions, is offered by Bank and Kahn (1982), who point out that, when one sibling is viewed as disabled, the non-disabled sibling will try and refrain from aggressive behaviour. The difficulty associated with this apparent 'good behaviour' is that the spontaneity of child play, including 'messing about', will be inhibited (Ibid. pp.259–60). Siblings may also be ashamed of or embarrassed by their disabled sibling and learn not to speak out, rather keeping their views to themselves, as this review has demonstrated. Consequently, it is not too surprising when Powell and Ogle (1985) note that siblings may feel confused about their role within the family, for they are both sibling and carer, playmate and responsible person, but without the maturity of an adult.

Life restrictions

In a survey carried out by Atkinson and Crawford (1995) for NCH Action for Children, seven out of ten children surveyed said their caring responsibilities placed restrictions on their lives. Richardson (1999), a brother with a disabled sister, could not remember being cared for himself; as he put it, ' I don't much recall being looked after'. His family had to focus on the needs of his disabled sister, as he did himself.

The consequences of having a disabled sibling are not all positive and I note adverse aspects too: for example, Janet aged 13, who has a sister with disabilities, said, 'I really do love my brothers and sister but they get so annoying I feel like crying' (Burke and Montgomery 2001b, p.38), demonstrating an important point, that other siblings can cause stress, for it is not necessarily a disabled sibling who may be cited when difficulties occur within the family.

Powell and Ogle (1985) suggest that siblings may feel confused about their role in the family, being both sibling and 'surrogate parent'. Furthermore, it is likely that siblings will not experience an equal freedom to go through the usual processes of childhood and adolescence, as experienced by non-disabled families, a process which, arguably, is the right of childhood. If sibling caretakers are denied both their childhood and their adolescence, it is likely that their needs will remain unmet and these require some attention during their experiences of carrying additional responsibilities for their disabled brothers or sisters.

According to Seligman (1991, p.184) research supports the notion that a sibling's responsibility for the disabled child may result in 'anger, resentment, guilt, and quite possibly, psychological disturbance'. Siblings with disabled brothers and sisters must first and foremost, be understood, and for that to happen, someone has to listen, and parents, as I have shown, are not always available to do so.

These illustrations, research findings and examples indicate the need for sibling support. Siblings of disabled brothers and sisters have a right not to talk about their feelings in the family. Indeed, some siblings do not seem aware that they have a right to their parents' time with the family focus being on the needs of the disabled child and the needs of other family members taking second place. The lack of communication in this and other families increases the non-disabled siblings' sense of isolation which sometimes comes near to despair.

The following case example was originally drawn from my earlier research (Burke and Cigno 2000) which began to identify the needs of siblings but, following my more recent findings, the initial analysis of the case is now developed in two ways: one, the locus of control is utilised as a significant means for determining the way Fay's life at home with Michael impacts on her school life and emotional wellbeing; and two, the idea of high positive reactive behaviour on the part of Fay is illustrated in her responses concerning Michael, and indeed, her family. The detail of the case is somewhat simplified to enable these points to be illustrated more clearly.

The case of Fay and Michael (high positive reaction)

Fay is 7 and her brother Michael is 5½ years old. At 18 months Michael was diagnosed as having a learning disability. He appeared not to notice pain, with the consequence that normally 'painful experiences', for example, running and tripping over, would not result in learning to be more careful. This means he is vulnerable and could cause himself a serious injury. Michael has attended special school from the age of 4. He also spent one weekend a month in respite care, which allowed more family time for Fay. Michael is affectionate towards his sister and they play happily together at home.

Fay has frequently been upset at school by comments from other children like 'your brother's stupid'. School friendships are difficult too because she will not tolerate jibes about her brother. Unfortunately, this approach has the effect of increasing rather than reducing the more intolerant behaviour from other school children.

Her parents feel she is being forced to mature earlier than her years should allow.

The locus of control

Examining Fay's circumstances concerning her 'locus of control' would suggest some confusion on Fay's part concerning her responsibilities towards her brother Michael. This is because Fay recognises that Michael is not able to accept responsibility for himself and consequently needs the protection of others: an external locus of control. In defending her brother, Fay tries to be the external control he needs, which seems part of her responsibility within the family. When other external forces seem to challenge her status, it appears she must rebuff them to retain her responsibilities as Michael's sister and carer. It is a simple dynamic of competing forces, but Fay, because of her age, does not have the skills to manage them and becomes distressed as a consequence, which leads to a positive over-reactive behaviour.

Positive over-reactive behaviour

This case example reflects on the growing evidence that children with disabilities and their siblings are bullied at school (Becker 2000; La Fontaine 1991); and particularly when brothers and sisters attend the same school and siblings come to the rescue of their brother or sister (Crabtree and Warner 1999). Bullying is taken seriously in most schools and Fay is suffering because of the attitude of other children in her school. Indeed, even her parents' attitude is that she is being forced to mature earlier, confirming her need to adopt a positive stance towards her brother; in other words she views her responsibilities as being protective of Michael's situation even in his absence, she will not accept criticisms of him directed at her by others, and she had become stigmatised as disabled by association in the process. She reacts by trying to defend her brother, but her behaviour may then be considered, at school, to be inappropriate, and she will suffer as a consequence. Fay needs support, and the behaviour of her peers needs changing. This might well require some action to be taken by Fay's teachers, who clearly need to do something to address the unacceptable attitudes of those children who bully others.

Conclusion

The needs of siblings should be considered equally with those of others in the family; but the right to express feelings must be recognised for all children. The role of professional workers must be to seek to enable the inclusion of siblings within family discussions and in the offering of service options, involving teachers, if necessary, as in the case of Fay. Services for the siblings of children with disabilities should offer some form of compensatory activities combined with the opportunity to discuss and share feelings.

It seems that there are dangers in viewing the care offered by siblings to their disabled brothers and sisters only as a positive benefit, since the evidence suggests that the needs of siblings may well be overlooked. The question of whether siblings take on a caring role willingly or grudgingly is unlikely to change their life course unless some form of professional intervention is made. It may well be that the identity of the caretakers is inseparable from that of their disabled sibling and that at some time in their lives, such as at the point of leaving home, for what ever reasons, the non-disabled sibling will need, at some emotional cost to themselves, to establish themselves as a person in their own right.

The framework for practice (Department of Health 2000a), it must be said, does recognise the needs of young carers, particularly when linked to the fact that local and health authorities may make an assessment of their ability to care, although, yet again, the central area of support links, in this context, to that of the child with disabilities. The needs of siblings should be considered equally with others within the family. The role of professional workers must be to seek to enable the inclusion of siblings within family discussions and in the offering of help, when needed, at school.

Chapter 6

Change, Adjustment and Resilience

The examination of the role of siblings so far has been explored in a reactive way to the situation they experience at home and school. In this chapter I consider how the accumulation of experience is potentially a life-changing event for siblings, given that their role is different from that of many of their peers and that the realisation of this is an important factor of their understanding and perception of family life. The title of the chapter summarises this experience of change, adjustment and resilience.

Change

Research shows that major changes induce stress because new experiences are often associated with challenge, uncertainty and fear of the unknown (Lazarus and Foulkman 1984), thus acknowledging that it is perfectly normal to experience an increase in stress when unexpected events are encountered. Middleton (1999) argues that change can bring about a positive identity. Moreover, a positive identity is about feeling good about oneself, 'acquiring identities relating to race, gender, age and appearance' (p.127), so that an identity acquired as a disabled person should involve an acceptance and public affirmation of self. This is also expressed by Wolfensberger (1998, p.119) who talks about 'adaptive identity' as a means for developing competencies in devalued groups, so that a socially acceptable status emerges, thus reducing the sense of difference and stigma associated with the devalued status. It is rather like the implementation of the social model when disability is not viewed as an individual problem;

rather the need is to ensure the integration and acceptance of people within the community. Change enables the process of adjustment to be accomplished: resilience is the capacity to make such an adjustment a positive experience. However, any adjustment is potentially stressful, and understanding the nature of stress helps an appreciation of the human condition.

Stress

Stress may be defined in any number of ways, but for our purposes it is about uncertainties that are faced when our routines are changed or challenged. According to Atkinson *et al.* (1990) stress occurs when we are unsure of our ability to deal with the event that are perceived as threatening. The Holmes and Rahe social readjustment scale (Hopson 1981) measures stress in terms of life changes to show that different life events are equated with higher or lower degrees of associated stress. Stressing events evaluated in a research study by Holmes and Rahe equated death of spouse at 100, change in the health of a family member scored 44, while personal injures scored 63, and it might be expected that most people routinely experience a mean stress level of 50. Various scores are attributed to events over a period of two years to assess the stress experienced by different individuals. These scores are intended to reflect the extent of stress experienced on an individual level. The higher the score the greater the likelihood of stress reactions: the greater the stressor, the greater the effort required to adapt to the stressing event.

ATTACHMENTS

The ability to deal with stress may link to the 'attachments' a child makes in early childhood, usually to a parent figure (Bowlby 1951; Rutter 1995), such attachments being thought to demonstrate what is referred to as 're-silience' which is not then a different concept. A child with good attachment experiences would be expected to be able to cope with changing situations, yet resilience can be seen to be different because it links to the ability to manage difficulties, including the ability to overcome adversity, the latter being the anthesis of attachment-forming experiences.

Reactions to stress may also evoke particular defence mechanisms as a form of protection against the unknown; as with bereavement, stress can numb our sense of understanding and impair our abilities to focus and understand situations.

DEFENCE MECHANISMS

My intention, unlike that of Holmes and Rahe (Hopson 1981), is not to evaluate whether one event is more or less stressing than another, but rather to suggest that accumulating stressful experiences will impact more on the individual involved. The nature of such an impact is of interest. Psychologists (Atkinson *et al.* 1990) tell us that coping with stress may be achieved through acquiring one or more of a number of defence mechanisms, without any necessary awareness of the process involved. Defence mechanisms are a form of avoidance, an unconscious handling of the stressing event, and the varying forms include: repression, an involuntary blocking-out of painful memories, rationalisation, finding an explanation for an event (which may or may not be logical), reaction formation (countering inner suspicions by an opposite reaction), projection (blaming others), intellectualisation (detachment achieved by dealing with the abstract), denial (avoidance of reality that any change has taken place) and displacement (finding another outlet for emotion, or interests).

There may be some element of overlap, for example, displacement could link to a reaction formation, although the point here is not to elaborate on the nature of defence mechanisms, but merely to clarify that it is a natural reaction to try and overcome difficulties which occur and which are stressful experiences to the recipient. The process of doing so can be partly explained by preparation for change, which may do much to help alleviate some, if not all, of the stress that change brings about.

In understanding stress, and the possibility of its accumulation, therefore, the Holmes and Rahe indications of reactions to lifestyle changes show that events other than bereavement may combine to increase the degree of stress experienced by the individual. This is not to say that siblings experience a bereavement because their brother or sister has a disability, but to suggest that because bereavement has been studied and understood it is helpful in accounting for the behaviour of siblings: to put it simply, looking at theories of bereavement help our understanding of stress reactions.

Adjusting to transitional stages

The Joseph Rowntree Foundation (http://www.jrf.org, 2002) identifies the need for transition planning for children with special needs, commenting that services are characterised by poor liaison between the different agencies, and 'the failure to involve young people in matters of the most importance to them and their families'. The message is that children should be involved in matters which concern them, not to do so is to increase the sense of stress that they already experience, externalising the locus of control and incapacitating a full adjustment to their situation.

Adjusting to accommodate the experience of stress or being stressed produces reactions of a defensive kind, which may vary according to the stage of 'bereavement' followed, that is, when the stress is sufficiently difficult to need overcoming. The process of overcoming high stress levels often results in transitional adjustments; for example, becoming a parent is a major transition, as is starting school, or indeed moving through childhood to adolescence.

The adjustment to caring for a child with disabilities is a transition for parents, but the experience of living with a brother or sister with disabilities may be a form of transition too, as differences are noted in the school playground between brothers and sisters, and remarks like ' your brother is mental, so are you' are hurtful and may not be received with tolerant and mature understanding, but require a resilient understanding of the behaviour of others. Research shows that transitions of any kind will cause stress (see Jones 1998) and in certain situations stress might be accommodated, but the nature of the transition must first of all be understood. However, resilience helps to explain why, when faced with apparently similar situations, people may react differently.

Resilience

The definition of resilience favoured by Daniel, Wassell and Gilligan (1999) is that used by Fonagy *et al.* which states that resilience is 'Normal development under difficult conditions (1994, pp.231–257). Werner's (1990) examination of international research on the subject indicates that resilient children elicit positive reactions from others. Resilient children have good communication skills, are sociable and independent. It seems that resilience enables adaptation to take place, so that an experience which renders one individual helpless, will in similar circumstances not faze another to the same degree: indeed it may confer a positive resolution of the difficulty. Gilligan (2001) indicates that children are shaped by a combination of potentially harmful and protective factors, where harmful equates with an element of risk, and protective factors include the situational support available within the family, suggesting that it is a combination of experiences which develops resilience.

Resilience, therefore, is the ability to manage difficult circumstances. This is exactly the situation of both siblings and children with disabilities when, as I found, parents express the view, 'they grow beyond their years', to explain the maturity and understanding that siblings of children with disabilities commonly share. It is a point clarified by French (1993), a woman with a visual disability, who discusses how, because of her awareness of the needs of others, she denied the reality of her disability to reduce the apparent anxiety and stress caused. French had previously discovered that, when she openly discussed her difficulties, would in doing so prompt disappointment, disbelief and disapproval, but by pretending to see what she could not, she engendered a sense of 'normality' and acceptance which avoided spoiling the fun of others by pretending to see what she could not. French would be asked, 'Can you see the colours of the rainbow?' She could not, but by a simple reply of 'yes', she gained approval from others. This is a form of denial but it is also part of interactive skills when dealing with others, putting on a 'brave face', facing one's own reality but not shoving it in other people's faces. It is exactly what resilience involves, adapting to situations without fuss and gaining approval in the process. It is a mechanism adopted by siblings who put the needs of others before themselves.

Putting others before one's self is somewhat routine for siblings who care for their disabled brother and sister, and who minimise their own needs to their parents. According to Dyson (1996), siblings will often face difficulties at school, find it difficult to bring friends home and, consequently, suffer loss of self-esteem. It appears that siblings find difficulty in forming attachments with other children because they feel stigmatised (Frude 1991). The research by Jenkinson (1998) found that negative attitudes at school tended to stereotype siblings of children with disabilities as different from their peers. This partly reflects the reality that a number of children have not encountered disability at school and do not know how to cope with it. Clearly, a child with resilient qualities will try to 'fit in', but such an adaptive process counts for little if perceptions of disability remain as a consequence, an unknown quantity to the 'normal' child. It suggests the need for 'inclusive' policies for disabled children in mainstream schools, but even then the difficulties may not be removed, as I found in the case of Henry described below.

The case of Robert and Henry (high positive reaction)

Henry is 6 years old and has an older brother, Robert, aged 8. Henry has poor co-ordination, uses a wheelchair, and attends a special school. Robert is confused by the fact that Henry goes to a special school and has not gone to his school, like other children with younger brothers. An added element to this perception of difference is the fact that another boy in his school uses a wheelchair like Henry's. Robert explained that Henry should be at his school and be 'the same' as the other boys. Yet, despite this belief, he says that he has not mentioned it to his mother because she 'must have her reasons'. Robert is showing concern for his brother and balances the needs of his mother against his own view of 'natural justice'. Perhaps Robert is right, but whether he will resolve his internal conflict of 'mother knows best' with his perception of the 'right school' remains unknown, and seems counter to the fact that as a boy reported to be doing rather poorly at school, he is demonstrating a level of understanding and awareness beyond his years. This is the beginning of resilience, and, as reflected by French (1993) in her discussion of denial, there is a deliberate avoidance of confrontation and a degree of collusion as a consequence. The opportunity to discuss such experiences is clearly Robert's right, for without it his sense is of powerlessness subject to the control of others.

Discussion

Most people have to work to a greater or lesser degree to accommodate change. It appears that brothers and sisters of disabled siblings may feel insecure. In a survey carried out by Atkinson and Crawford (1995), seven out of ten children surveyed said their caring responsibilities placed restrictions on their lives: such perceptions make for differences when making self-comparisons with one's peers. At school siblings may feel different because their situation at home does not compare directly with the experience of others. It is not surprising, therefore, that the transitions they are required to make, despite any coping skills of a resilient kind, can have a negative effect on their perceptions of fairness. This is the situation of Robert discussed above.

In another example reported in my research (Burke and Montgomery 2003) Sarah, aged 12, would look after and play with her disabled sister. When friends called and ask her to go out with them, she had to refuse because of her responsibilities towards her sister. This caring responsibility is described by Allott (2001) who reports a discussion she had with 10-year-old Laura. Laura helps to look after her older brother who has 'something wrong with his back and legs and he can't walk'. Laura gets her brother dressed in the mornings and feels she has to 'care for him a lot'. It seems that whether siblings take on a caring role willingly or reluctantly it will impact on their perceptions of what is reasonable and fair. The non-disabled sibling needs to have a right of expression, to assert their own rights as individuals, because as children, no matter how maturely they learn to behave, they lack the opportunity to be treated as others because their needs are not understood. Mayhew and Munn (1995, p.38), express concern that 'conforming and altruistic response' should be as worrying as 'acting-out behaviour'. Certainly, a greater acceptance by others is required, but for that to happen, the needs of siblings have to be recognised as part of the process. Unfortunately, the reality is that such needs are all too easily ignored, resulting in isolation and exclusion from the world of other children.

These illustrations and examples indicate the need for sibling support. Siblings of disabled brothers and sisters have a right not to talk about their feelings in the family, but the situations reported above appear to reflect: (i) the lack of opportunity to talk abut their feelings; (ii) a consequent lack of recognition concerning their needs; and (iii) assumptions that siblings are treated the same as other children. Indeed, some siblings do not seem aware that they have a right to their parents' time with the family focus being on the needs of the disabled child and the needs of other family members seemingly less important. The lack of communication in this and other families increases when the non-disabled siblings' sense of isolation is compounded by experiences at home and at school. This can result in an acute despair caused by misunderstanding and uncertainty on the part of the sibling. One feeling, which was consistently expressed, was that of embarrassment, an examination of which should provide some insight into the needs of siblings themselves.

Embarrassment

A feeling, which is common among siblings, is that of embarrassment. Richardson (1999) writes about his family experience, saying 'Embarrassment was never far behind. You start to feel somehow 'disabled' yourself, or to wish that you were'. This rather suggests that, in his situation, his disabled sibling was unaware that her actions might draw attention to herself, actions which he felt were probably considered unusual by others, making him wish he was less conscious and less aware of the differences himself. His perceptions of the construction that others placed on what 'is normal' pervaded his own intellect and became a form of anguish over which he had no control, hence the wish that he too could be disabled in a similar way to his sister. In this example, becoming disabled would make him like his sister, and so he would also be unaware of the differences others perceived and which, with his present awareness, he interpreted as a painful consequence, simply expressed here as embarrassment.

The experience of embarrassment has other manifestations, as Frank (1996) writes and in agreement with Dyson (1996), indicating that siblings may feel unable to bring friends home or take their disabled brother or sister out in public, because of embarrassment about appearance or health needs of the disabled sibling. Meadows (1986) expresses sibling reaction as involving a range of interactions, from simple embarrassment, to reacting aggressively or in an 'out-of-control' way. Such responses would fit rather neatly with a type of bereavement cycle as siblings make continual adjustments on a daily basis. It seems that siblings are acutely aware of the differences they perceive in their disabled brother or sister and distance themselves from situations which highlight those differences.

In my own discussions with two groups of siblings (with eight siblings in each group, carried out to compare group responses with individual ones), the views expressed by Sarah, aged 12, were fairly typical. She explained that when she was out with her family and her brother, Matthew aged 8, he would sometimes shout and sit on the pavement and not move; Sarah would move away and pretend she was not with him, waiting for him to calm down. Sarah helped clarify the issue by saying that when she went shopping with her family, including Matthew, other people would stare, as if in disbelief, at his odd behaviour. This had the effect of making the family feel they were somehow irresponsible for allowing their son to behave in a socially unacceptable way. The reality is that Matthew's behaviour is acceptable to the family and Matthew would not understand that his behaviour is other than ordinary. Embarrassment seemed to be a reaction to events out of the ordinary, as when another child recalled, 'my brother ran into my class at school in just his underwear'. Perhaps the sense of embarrassment is simply related to unpredictable behaviour, whether by the sibling themselves, or on the part of the public. It seems that a socially conditioned response by the family would be to stop going out, and that would exclude any opportunity for a 'normal' family life through self-imposed isolation: it should not be a choice anyone should have to make, although it will take a major re-education of the public to gain a greater acceptance of families with disabled children.

The emotional responses of siblings towards their disabled brothers and sisters are not all negative. Feelings of embarrassment are not uncommon; other reactions are also evident (and my findings echo those of Connors and Stalker 2003, p.82), and some of these are positive in their association with siblings.

Positive responses

The majority of younger siblings interviewed (out of 22) had mainly positive feelings about their disabled brothers and sisters. Debbie, aged 8, played happily with her brother Sam, aged 4, particularly play-fighting providing Sam's boots were taken off. Sam will attend the same school as Debbie and she has already been told to expect to help to look after him at break times. Sam has bitten Debbie but because she cannot bear to see him upset she does not respond. She already accepts that he is not fully responsible for his actions and makes appropriate allowances, demonstrating a growing awareness of his needs and the probable reactions of others. However, whether she should be coached into a caretaker role at school, despite her apparent acceptance that this would be a responsibility placed on her, is a debatable point. This illustrates that a positive reaction can have consequences which are not always desirable for someone who has a right to their own independence rather than being cast into a caretaker role from an early age.

The situation of Angela, aged 12, clarifies her reactions to her brother John, aged 9, when she allows herself to be angry with him but is able to control her anger: 'Sometimes I just grab him...I make a fight a game', and so displaces her anger in a positive way. It may be that Debbie lacks such an opportunity, which may lead to difficulties when Sam starts attending the same school (see case reported in Chapter 1).

In the following case, drawn from interviews with family members, it will be evident that living with a child with a disability makes a difference to siblings in terms of their play and choice of leisure activities, but that difference is matched by a clear attachment and acceptance of disability within the family, even though the encounters with friends and neighbours means that the reaction of embarrassment is never too far beneath the surface.

The case of Victoria, Jenny and Paul (low positive reaction)

Victoria, aged 11 years, lives in a large comfortable terraced house in a small village in East Yorkshire. She is cared for by her mother and shares her home with her sister and brother, Jenny, aged 15 and Paul, aged 13.

Mother reports that she felt that something was different about Victoria from the age of 8 months. At 2 years of age Victoria seemed indifferent to attention from adults, a matter first mentioned by her. However, the diagnosis of 'autism' was not suspected and would only be confirmed when Victoria reached the age of 9. At the time of writing she attends a special school, does homework and enjoys working on the computer. She has to be spoken to in the third person to ensure understanding. For example, saying 'would you please' will not get a response, but saying, 'Would Victoria please…' usually gets her attention. Victoria sings obsessively and, as is common with all her behaviour, she has a compulsion for order. This is reflected in one of her special skills; she is very accurate at spelling, and is well in advance of her years.

Family outings, however, are said to be very stressful, particularly if Victoria has to be stopped from running around in and out of shops, across the road, or when she indulges in screaming fits; all of which makes people stare. Such is her need for order that everything has to be explained to her in advance before she is taken out otherwise she will resort to screaming tantrums. Even when she eats she eats symmetrically: from alternate sides of a sandwich to make a regular pattern. Her preference for order is particularly reflected in her enjoyment of 'MacDonald's' burgers, which are of predictable consistency wherever the location.

Both Jenny and Paul said they spent most of their leisure time at home, Jenny watching television and Paul on the 'Playstation'. Jenny has a part-time job at weekends. Paul spends most of his time at home. At home Jenny sometimes finds it difficult to manage the stress caused by Victoria. One illustration of this was when Victoria changed some project work, of which Jenny was very proud, and had altered incorrect spellings to make the project perfect (to Victoria), but spoiling the presentation of the work as a result, much to Jenny's dismay. Jenny explained that she 'get used to things like that', and that it 'does not bother too much', although clearly experiencing some initial upset.

Regarding his relationship with Victoria, Paul said that sometimes he had more trouble with his older sister, but with Victoria he had to be aware that she would easily embarrass him because of her lack of understanding of normal behaviour. One problem Paul had with Victoria followed her discovery of a way of wiping out his saved 'Playstation' games after he had played for several hours, and her apparent indifference to what she had done. Also, he felt his home life was restrictive because he could not bring friends home, and was unable to get out as much as he would like. His view of life with Victoria was expressed as follows:

> Life would be easier without her, but if I had a magic wand I wouldn't make her any different, otherwise she wouldn't be Victoria. I'd keep her the way she is; otherwise she could end up like Jenny (grinning as he mentioned his older sister's name).

It appears that Paul has a well-adjusted view of his family and accepts with good humour the limitations he experiences in comparisons with his peers. He can express his difficulties as he encounters them, as does his sister Jenny. Paul and Jenny appear to have some measure of resilience concerning the transitions they face. Their adjustment tends to be typified by a low positive response (see Table 2.1 (4)), treating Victoria with some caution in order to maintain a quiet life. It is probably an important factor that the family live in a small village, where Victoria's differences are accepted, so that the family is not stigmatised for being different and where the boundaries of the local community help to promote a positive view of life at home.

The case of Alan and Mary (compliant reaction)

In this example, an adult sibling, Alan, has learnt a form of compliant behaviour due to the frequent absences of his sister, Mary, from the family home. Mary had severe learning disabilities with challenging behaviour since childhood and by the time she and her brother both reached their early 20s they had led almost separate lives. Mary was sent to a residential school in her teenage years and continues to reside away from the family home. For the greater part of her life she has been apart from the family except to return home for specific holiday periods. This distancing in the relationship, caused by infrequent meetings, led to later difficulty for Alan to acknowledge, socially, the existence of his sister.

In this example, it appears that the simple lack of acknowledgement stems from infrequent contacts between siblings as younger people, although in the case of John and James (Chapter 3), the distancing there came from a significant age gap with the disabled child being the younger in the family.

Comment

The importance of support for families with a disabled child should be recognised. Family support includes both informal community support such as that given by friends and neighbours, and special support services (Burke and Cigno 1996; 2000). It should also include support offered to siblings, whose needs are explored in this study. However, support from specialist services may help siblings like Jenny and Paul, and in the next chapter the role of the support group is examined to see whether it actually facilitates the type of help required.

Chapter 7

The Role of Sibling
Support Groups

It is a fact, according to Frude (1991) that siblings of children with disabilities have greater insight into the needs of others. Reaction to disabilities results in some families becoming more united, while others find the stress of caring responsibilities difficult to manage. In the previous chapter I discussed the characteristics of resilience as an aspect of the developmental experience of siblings, but such characteristics cannot be assumed to be there, even though it would seem that sibling experiences will promote them. How then can siblings be helped to deal with the various transitions that they face on a regular basis?

This chapter reflects on the experience of attending a support group to show how this may help siblings to forge an identity, seek help from others and become mutually supportive. The chapter concludes with a consideration of five key questions which may be asked about a support group. Indeed, in summary, it is apparent that attendance at a support group will often help siblings to express their feelings in an environment that is free of the daily 'embarrassing encounters' that tend to typify part of the daily routine of siblings.

The need for support
According to Gardner and Smyle (1997) support should be provided wherever it is needed. This is an uncontentious comment but it serves to

indicate that support, help or assistance is a recognised way of responding to need. The qualification of need with regards to siblings, according to Frank, Newcomb and Beckman (1996), is in providing opportunities to reduce emotional stress and isolation. This is achieved by promoting the development of coping strategies in dealing with day-to-day situations.

The role played by sibling support groups can do much to help coping strategies to develop, often by simply making time available for young people to express their feelings and experiences in a safe environment. Richardson (1999) suggests that siblings need support groups to help them to understand the realities of disabilities because siblings are adept at denying their own needs. Barr (1999) suggests that siblings need counselling to help reduce anxieties and stress. It seems logical to suggest that, although support may have many manifestations, including individual one-to-one help, the idea of a support group for siblings appears to be a successful way of dealing with sibling needs. A support group may ensure that peer relationships are developed, which then enables a journey of self-discovery.

The initial findings from the pilot study on sibling support (Burke and Montgomery 2001a), involved eight families, all of whom agreed that the experience of attending a sibling support group was a good experience for everyone. In the survey within the main stage of the research a siblings group was rated on a scale from 1 to 5, 5 being very helpful, 3 neither helpful or unhelpful and 1 not very helpful (but see appendix for a more detailed methodology). All 41 families whose children attended the siblings group were asked to rated the group within the survey question-naire (Burke and Montgomery 2003) and 38 families rated the group meetings as either very helpful or fairly helpful, of whom 33 rated the group very helpful, and 5 as fairly helpful. Three families did not complete the rating question. The response from siblings themselves (16 from group interview, and 10 within individual interviews) echoed this finding; in particular, the opportunity to meet on a regular basis was generally welcomed as an enjoyable experience. This confirmed the trend first identified within the pilot study and demonstrates that, when siblings attend a support group, they value the experience and benefit from it: it does not show that all support groups are valued in the same way, although this one was certainly appreciated by parents completing the questionnaire and by siblings who were interviewed independently (at the group session held at the Family Centre).

Indeed, even when a sibling group was not available (for the 15 families in the control group) all responses (from parents) were in favour of group support being offered. It should be evident then that, whether or not families had children attending a support group, all favoured the opportunity for additional activities. In only one case was there a rejection of the sibling group and that was based on an initial bad first experience; even then, the child concerned expressed the view that 'it must be fun if you like that kind of thing (10-year-old girl on out-door adventure activities).

In order to expand on the reactions of membership of the siblings group and provide a qualitative reflection on the data concerning attendance, the experience of Peter and Ian is helpful to recount.

The case of Peter and Ian (low negative reaction)

Peter is 14 and has a younger disabled brother Ian, aged 10. Ian goes to a special school for physically disabled young people. Peter attends a sibling support group. He says that he enjoys the sibling group experience, but freely admitted that he had not kept in contact with any of the other young people that attended with him. He liked meeting people and the activities that were followed, but apart from mentioning an interest in computers he could not say what actually happened when he went to the group sessions. He was able to express his feelings about the organisation of the groups and explained that weekly sessions were arrange for periods running for eight weeks, and sometimes these were planned twice a year, although the next group of sessions were, as far as Peter was aware, still in the planning stage. He said his parents would receive a letter to tell them when the group would run again, but he had no idea when that would be.

Apart from the siblings group, Peter said he had no friends locally, a situation that seemed not to bother him, perhaps if so he would not make such an admission. Much of his time at home was spent on the computer when it was available. He also said that he got into fights with his younger brother, Ian, despite his disability, but more often fighting involved 'fighting-back, as needed' rather than starting the fight himself. Peter seems to be a bit of a loner, a seemingly not uncommon reaction to disability in the family (echoing Joe mentioned in Chapter 4), and as he expresses it, he made the decision 'not see my school friends after school', thus keeping his home life separate from his school experiences.

Peter explained that because his brother Ian attends a different school he felt it was better not to let children in his school know about him. Peter's home life and school experiences are separate life events and even the siblings group is treated as an experience which only exists during the duration of attendance, so the pattern of no follow-up of friendships reflects a choice Peter has made. Peter has a life which is of a rather remote kind, a compartmental, but not a fully isolating experience, yet lacking any integration between the differing experiences. He explains that while at school he 'felt like a "geek" but that was better than being the 'known' brother of a disabled child with other children 'being stupid' about it. It is as though his behaviour minimises the effect of disability by association by effectively taking steps to exclude its impact.

Behaviour

Peter has a low negative type of reaction to his situation; he lets things happen, but avoids over-involvement. It is negative because he avoids confrontation in order to maintain some minimal control over his life, but this is based on an assumption that somehow disability is not acceptable in his life. This suggests that events like school and the siblings-group, even, indeed, his play-fighting with his brother – are influenced by external factors, because they are events over which he has little say; his reaction is not to seek any link between situations, so no transfer of friendships takes place, which suggests that Peter's life is restricted by his perceptions of disability, which is in itself disabling. This behaviour is not a strong reaction against disability, because Peter expresses the wish, effectively through inactivity, to keep situations as they are. Yet he does not wish to be identified as the brother of a disabled sibling, which is a denial of his sibling relationship. It would certainly be an area for discussion within the protective environment of the sibling support group.

The need for self-expression

One of the main benefits of attending a siblings group, as reported by Burke and Montgomery (2003), was expressed by a 14-year-old boy who said:

> It's good to meet everyone else with a disabled brother or sister. People on the street don't understand – some people call my sister names – that does not happen in the siblings group.

The comment 'people in the street don't understand' rings true, given the experience of Peter above and might help explain the reluctance, certainly of some siblings, to challenge the experience of rejection by others. In Peter's case perhaps his avoidance of situations excludes the possibility of a rejection or 'name calling' experience and enables him to pursue a quiet life undisturbed by others who do not have the knowledge of his situation at home. However, the siblings group itself provides a safe environment for brothers and sisters to be treated as equals, given a shared understanding of the impact of disability on their respective lives. Membership of the siblings group is not always easily achieved, as siblings new to the group have to learn to identify with the shared understanding achieved by others.

Although the evidence is overwhelmingly in favour of attending a sibling support group, the experience of attendance is not without stress and, as reported in Burke and Montgomery (2001b), the process of joining a group results in a degree of uncertainty at what to expect and, although only one young person rejected the group through being put off by the prospect of being involved in outdoor activities, the stress of starting something new should not be underestimated.

Initial stress on joining a group

Joining a sibling support group will often result in an initial sense of stress arising from the transition to a new situation. Also, the siblings group has a specific membership, based on having a disabled sibling, and giving a sense of 'exclusivity' which might not be perceived in a totally positive way by new members, uncertain of their status and feeling at the beginning of an introduction to a new 'pecking order' of seniority. This may be because of experiences elsewhere which induce a sense of isolation following encounters with the public which may confer a negative identity as the brother or sister of a disabled child. Such experiences make siblings feel different, prompting them to ask questions of their parents, such as 'Why can't I be like everyone else?' However, once the initial stress of transition is overcome (arising from a lack of confidence that the situation will be any different from experiences at school or even at home), membership of the sibling group may begin to reduce the sense of isolation experienced by siblings.

Through talking about their disabled brothers and sisters and their experiences siblings will soon realise they share similar experiences with the other members of the group. Two quotes from group members illustrate the point:

> It's nice to know other people have brothers and sisters with disabilities. You kind of think no one else has disabled brothers and sisters. You can talk with other children and find out what their lives are like.
>
> Phillipa, aged 13

> The siblings group helps you to realise you're not the only one; other people have brothers and sisters like you.
>
> Anne, aged 15

Membership of the group helped promote a common identity about experiences which might often be thought to be unique within the family. Overcoming the initial stress on joining the group was quickly replaced with a realisation that the group was helpful to individual young people. For these children, being around others who understood how they felt was a very positive aspect of being in the group. The sharing and comparing of experiences was a liberating opportunity for most young people but required the protection and security of the group to facilitate discussion.

Sometimes friendships formed continued beyond the duration of the group sessions, but even when they did not, as illustrated by Peter above, they were still considered valuable. One boy said:

> When I'm out with her (his younger disabled sister) people stare at us, as if it's their fault that she is the way she is, in the group people accept you, you are not different or strange, it feels normal.
>
> Mark, aged 15

Clearly, siblings value the group, and one of the main reasons they do so is because it confers an identity which, despite its origins, for siblings with disabled brothers and sisters establishes their rights as individuals who do not need to be overwhelmed by being a relative of a disabled person. The siblings group was liked because, according to two siblings, it was away from home and away from the daily encounter with disability. It does seem that experiences in the siblings group are free of the expected judgements of others, and because of that it is recognised as a relatively unique experience. The experience of being the sibling of a disabled person confers to some degree the stigma of being disabled by association, as experienced in daily interactions with others, even though such stigmatisation should not happen. These views, as expressed to me, highlight the fact that the group offered some sort of break from family life and because of that it was highly valued by those who took the opportunity of attending.

What siblings liked about group experiences

For a siblings group to be successful, according to the siblings interviewed for the research, they would like: a professional facilitator; age-related groups; fixed and regular times when meetings occur; activity weekends; and, perhaps most important, time when they would be listened to, either one-to-one with a facilitator or in group discussion time.

Siblings groups should provide time for sharing experiences and opportunities for mutual support: this finding is echoed by an American organisation called The ARC (a national organisation on mental retardation) in its web page (http://www.thearc.org/faqs/siblings.html revised February 2000) which offers detailed advice to families and professionals. It identifies the fact that siblings of brothers and sisters with disabilities experience challenges that other families may not experience, which then impact on the sibling's development and their attitude towards others. It is for this reason that siblings groups are helpful; they enable siblings to reinforce their identity as 'special' in the sense of the experiences they can share within the group.

The ARC provides a comprehensive programme of support activities, including a siblings forum, family support with respite care to enable families to experience short-term breaks from their caring responsibilities, and services within an integrated setting where all siblings can become involved. A directory of sibling services is available, which extends to adult siblings of people with special needs. However, in Britain services are still developing and are not so comprehensive, hence the need to comment on the sibling group, which was specifically evaluated for this text.

All siblings who have a brother or sister with a disability or special needs are likely to need some support from others who share similar experiences. A series of five 'who, when and how' questions now follows, which should help sibling group facilitators to reflect on the structure, membership and organisation of the group. The theory on group process will often discuss the need for leadership (Corey 2004) as recognition of the specialised skills that are required. The term preferred here, however, is 'group facilitator', which is used to signify that activities are a joint enterprise between the facilitator and group members and reinforces the fact that the group's activities are linked directly to the input from its members.

Who should attend?

A support group is necessary because its existence provides recognition of the fact that families with children with disabilities may find it difficult to provide the attention siblings need owing to the focus on the child with disabilities. A support group provides time and space for siblings to be more egocentric; their needs are central to the purpose and function of the group's activities. In families where more than one sibling is eligible to attend a group it may generate ambivalent feelings if they both belong to the same group. The sibling group needs to enable siblings to foster their own identity, which suggests separate group experiences might help in this, the issue being about one's identity being subsumed by the needs of the other, so that a younger sibling may feel out of place if undertaking group activities with an older brother or sister. This might even mirror the situation at home with the younger child taking second place.

In interview, Sarah, aged 12, had moved up into the next age group leaving her younger sibling behind; age banding may be necessary but should not be totally restrictive, especially should a brother and sister wish to stay together. Yet, the sensitivities of siblings are such that they may say the right thing to accommodate a sibling's feelings at the expense of their own, which is reflected by the comment made by Jane, aged 14, when she said, 'I liked being with Sarah (her younger sister) in the group but it was better when I had the group to myself.' This is clearly not hard evidence of group functioning, but professionally it makes sense to consider the needs of each sibling and not to conflate the needs of a brother and sister together as one simply because they are from the same family.

What age groups?

A finding from the evaluation of the siblings group was that siblings were concerned about the age of members within the group. Some siblings felt uncomfortable when the age range of the group was too broad. Teenagers were not especially delighted to be put into pre-teen groups. Younger siblings liked sessions to be focused on their age range of interests and fundamental to this was being given a choice rather than having imposed sessions, otherwise, 'I could be at school – following a course for GCSE.' Age-appropriate sessions are needed, facilitated by a group leader with whom the group can identify, and one way of achieving that is to help the group to make choices about which activities are to be followed.

What kind of activities?

Siblings enjoyed the sense of free choice in pursuing activities within group sessions organised on their behalf by the siblings' group facilitator. The younger ones liked the spacious environment of the clubroom; all age groups enjoyed art-related activities which enabling creative energies to be expressed. Other activities, such as weekend outdoor pursuits were seen as the sort of exciting challenge, which would not necessarily be possible within their families. Outdoor experiences mentioned were caving, abseiling, horse riding, sleeping in a tent and orienteering. It is clearly important that when opportunities are provided for siblings the purpose is to enable them to express themselves through the new experiences. Having a say in what is available, perhaps through providing a menu of activities to encourage the flexibility of group choice enables preferences to be established. However, facilitators should not have a restrictive menu and need be open to new ideas and suggestions expressed by the group. Inevitably, some restrictions might apply, like when a sibling suggested a group trip to Australia, which lay beyond the means of the group to arrange, even though many warmed to the idea. The scale and scope of suggestions need to be realistic and possible, otherwise disappointments can only result.

How often?

It is clear that the siblings group is seen as a valuable resource, but it needs to be available on a regular basis. The group under evaluation only met on a weekly sessional basis over an eight-week period. Different groups met at different times of the year. An activity weekend was planned for all siblings regardless of which eight-week block they joined. This meant activities were compressed within the block of time allocated to the groups and were somewhat frenetic, especially if they included a weekend activity-based project.

All siblings encountered within the two group sessions (eight siblings each from all groups) that form part of the evaluation said they would prefer to meet on a regular basis, even once a month, rather than every week during the eight-week life of the group. Such an approach would provide a sense of continuity and help foster a club-like atmosphere rather than a 'quick-fix' and necessarily highly organised approach. No matter how good the latter might be, siblings need the opportunity to meet more often rather than less, and again it is an issue of choice, listening to those who participate within the groups. In a way this demonstrates that sibling have continuing needs, which should be responded to and identified at the point when help is needed rather than being delayed because a group might not reconvene for another six months.

The issue is a serious one, because the value of the group will diminish for those that most need it, if it is only offered at a minimal level of attendance levels because of the excessive demand for the service. Rationing in such a context may do more harm than good. It was generally considered better to have a regular meeting to look forward to than the uncertainty of not knowing when the next group session might begin.

The need for regular meetings is echoed by the experience of Peter, whose situation is the subject of the case example earlier in this chapter, and who led a life with rather separated experiences despite a commitment to the group. Improving the sense of continuity of the group might encourage stronger friendships to develop, which extend beyond the group, and possibly lead to the seemingly impossible achievement of being able to invite a friend to one's home.

What about parental responsibilities?

There seemed to be a lack of clarity reflected in interviews with parents, concerning what was involved within the individual group sessions themselves. Parents said that they understood that it was their children's time, which their children needed for themselves, and as such parental involvement might be construed as an intrusion and consequently undermine the sense of 'membership' felt by siblings. Naturally, parental involvement was perceived by parents as only existing at a minimal level of input apart from simply being required to agree their siblings' attendance at the group. In such circumstances parents become, understandably, a little mystified concerning the activities involved, except when further agreement is sought, as required when involving siblings in 'away-day' activity weekends.

Parents do need some feedback from the group facilitators to ensure that what goes on has their approval, and their perception is that this does not happen. It is fundamental to the legal concept of 'parental responsibilities' that parenthood is concerned with a child's 'moral, physical and emotional health' (Herbert 1993, p.3) and as such should safeguard the welfare of the child. When young people are engaged in activities beyond the home, parents need to know the nature of such activities. Within a sibling's group this implies some form of reporting back to reassure parents that all is well, as might be assumed when the child is at school and professionals act *in loco parentis*, as it were, taking the place of parents in their absence.

A form of syllabus which included the requirement to determine the ascertainable wishes and feelings of the child might meet this need, perhaps combined with an attendance certificate that recognises an achievement by a particular child.

Comment

It is evident that attending a siblings group is of benefit to the siblings involved because siblings are, perhaps for the first time, in a group where they are not different from others. Simply having a disabled brother or sister confers membership of the group. Despite some initial stress through the novelty of the experience, siblings soon learn, to enjoy the atmosphere of common understanding which exists within the group examined. Siblings may not wish to talk about themselves but should they wish to, someone will listen. One of the main findings from the research is that siblings gain a voice by attending a group, which enables them to be honest about themselves, to express their fears, anxieties and wishes for the future with other young people who understand, usually other siblings, or a professional facilitator as the need arises.

The professional role in facilitating such groups is of considerable importance, since it enables a positive identity to be gained by siblings, substituting for one which may have had negative images of disability arising from a sense of difference. It is important to recognise, too, that sibling groups are not just about activities and, while siblings should have a say in those activities which are undertaken and demonstrate their ability to choose in the process, the objective of any group is to reinforce feelings of identify and self-worth, so that encounters with others are no longer defensive, but siblings can be proud to have a brother or sister with disabilities, knowing that their experiences are special. Indeed, much of the research cited tends to confirm that siblings become more mature, caring and well-adjusted individuals as consequences of their experiences. The siblings group aids that process during the frequent uncertainties of adolescence and helps that enhanced development to be realised while minimising the stresses of childhood with which disability is often associated.

It does seem that group experiences are different from those encountered at home: at home life is too focused, too different, for siblings to gain a perspective, yet not everyone will seek attendance at a sibling group, and the message should be noted that, while a sibling support group will be useful for many (and its organisation may be of some significance here), not everyone will choose to benefit from it and the siblings group should not be the only answer simply because it is successful. Some siblings will need some individual form of special attention. For such children, professional workers may need to offer or facilitate one-to-one attention offering it as a natural development without increasing the sense of needing special help or reinforcing, as it were, feelings of difference in needing help. It may be that for such isolated children disability is perpetuated by an accumulation of discriminations, as occurs with race, gender and low socio-economic status, a layering effect that can lead to withdrawal and isolation.

It is clear, however, that children need to communicate their feelings to others, to explain their fears and frustrations, since only then will they overcome the apparent sense of disadvantage and stigma that others impose. This is an individual view, but another agenda concerns the societal levels of pressures that discriminate against people viewed as different, when difference should be celebrated and not viewed as a cause for embarrassment, as so often reported in this research. The next chapter begins to move beyond the individual to the broader concerns of empowerment.

Chapter 8

Support Services and Being Empowered

A central concern within this book is the need to respect the wishes and feeling of young people. This raises the ethical issues of whether children are involved in discussions that concern them, directly or indirectly, because not contributing to such discussion is effectively excluding their contribution (Connors and Stalker, 2003, p.101). I view this as retaining the power to make a decision over and above the wishes of the child: indeed parents will make such decisions routinely as responsible parents and may, without thought or regard, exclude the child's view (Burker and Cigno 2000).

In the field research which informs this book permission to interview a child first of all required parental agreement, and when that was given, at the stage of interviewing the child, the child's agreement was sought before an interview could take place. This sets a model for practice, to include the child whenever possible when decisions are taken. It is exactly the situation reported in an earlier work (Burke and Cigno 2001), when, in the context of professional practice, to make decisions that concerned a disabled child without including them in the decision-making process not only ignores the child's wishes and feelings as represented within the Children Act 1989, it is also a form of exclusion which is simply oppressive.

Communicating needs

Communicating needs is an interactive process: first, one has to listen and understand, second, one has to express needs, often to people with the power to meet them, and, third, one responds to offers to meet needs. It is a continuing process as refining one's understanding is clarified by further discussion. I have referred to the communication of needs without the agreement of the child as advocacy by unauthorised proxy (Burke and Cigno 2001). This results when an interpretation of need is made without proper consultation, which may be called the 'I know best' approach, one that does not wait to check the views or opinions of others on the matter. Fitton (1994) examined the carer's responsibility based on her personal experience, expressing the view that when interpreting a child's needs a protective stance is a common reaction, which is not always in the child's best interest. Siblings can often offer an alternative view in such circumstances, reflecting a more positive outlook to challenges carers may seek to minimise.

The situation of siblings of children with disabilities is often somewhat distant from the decisions which concern their disabled brother or sister, and their needs may not be fully taken into account. There is a danger that siblings can easily be overlooked in the desire to meet the needs of the disabled child. This may easily transpire when children expect their parents or carers to make decisions on their behalf. In most cases parents are the best advocates for and protectors of their children, but this is not always the case, and professionals may sometimes focus more firmly on parents' than on children's needs (Welch 1998), leaving the disabled child and siblings in something of a backwater regarding their own needs.

In an example mentioned by a parent in a research interview, one practitioner apparently expressed this view of a sibling in an assessment-based interview.

> Well, Mary as you are 13 now, and independent, you need not worry about all of this. You can leave the room if you wish, because this does not concern you.

The situation under discussion concerned her brother who had severe physical disabilities and who relied on his sister as a playmate, helper and confidante. All such matters were summarily dismissed because the focus of attention was on disability and not on the consequences for her sibling, a situation made worse by the fact that both parents were included while Mary had to leave the room. One way of addressing the issue is to clarify the process of communicating needs for all concerned. However, there are no easy ways to incorporate the views of those whose communicative abilities are not well understood or expressed and whose needs are dependent on others.

In my research (Burke and Cigno 1996; Burke 1998) it was demonstrated that the needs of children with learning disabilities might be subsumed in the wishes of more verbally able individuals, usually parents, who articulate these needs for their children. The effect, if not the intent, may be the exclusion of the wishes and feelings of the children themselves. It is worth repeating, however, that parents of children with disabilities, like other parents, are likely to be inextricably bound up in the health and welfare of their children and have their best interests at heart but, as in the case of the social worker mentioned above, this should not mean that the children of the family are excluded from the assessment discussions.

It is also possible that, under the additional stresses of caring, the parent's perceptions of their child's needs and wishes might become confused with their own needs as parents. There is a danger, therefore, of making assumptions which makes children experience a form of social exclusion through a kind of omission, an unwitting and unintentional lack of consideration. In attempting to unravel the complexities of the interactions which exist between child, carer and professional, the need to consider the child's voice provides a way forward.

Communication: The child's voice

An individual's need to achieve the right to choose is endorsed by the National Health Services and Community Care Act 1990. With reference to children this was underpinned by the United Nations Convention on the Rights of the Child (1989) when in 1992 the UK government agreed to be bound by the convention. This requires that children have the right to express an opinion, a basic entitlement referred to in terms of their freedom of expression (article 12). It is also a matter of law: in Britain the

Children Act 1989 makes clear that the views of children must be sought over decisions concerning their health and welfare. Children, therefore, have a legal right to have a say in matters that affect them.

The problem for many children with disabilities is that they may not be able to express their views in conventional ways, and parents generally act as their child's proxy by stating his or her interests as they see them. I am doing exactly this in writing about my research. The issue which has to be addressed concerns the mechanisms by which the rights and welfare of children translate into a greater efforts to include them in decision-making relevant to their needs.

Interestingly, some lessons can be learned from the research process referred to in Chapter 2 where the issue of the acceptability of a child's account of events is acceptable. It seems that such views concern a Court's understanding of what constitutes acceptable evidence from a child. Clearly, what children say about their situation is valid and their perspective is vitally important; it should not follow that a child's view is always and necessarily evidentially based and it must, therefore, meet rigid criteria before achieving acceptance. Nonetheless, the child has a right to express an opinion and to make a choice, and should always be encouraged by workers.

The matter of exploitation is more difficult to counter, because present and future vulnerability and long-term damage are harder to quantify or predict. Even here, the issue might be resolved by taking greater care with the research approach adopted in order to minimise any possibility of increasing the child's vulnerability by overactively engaging them in research. This may raise the question of contaminated data: whose view is being ascertained, the child's or the interviewer's? This is a matter concerning the capacity to give true consent (Law Commission 1995). Such issues are commonplace for practitioners, who regularly encounter problems in communicating with children with special needs and interpreting their wishes.

The role of the professional and empowerment

The responsible professionals should recognise the rights of people, including children, to have a say in matters that concern them. This requires the integration of siblings within professional assessments of need within community care, especially when making assessments of family situations. The ecological approach within assessment procedures will enable the voice of children to be heard. There is a need to move towards acceptance and recognition of families with disabled children and their siblings, which Finkelstein (1993, p.15) refers to as 'control over their lives'. Control in this sense may include a political dimension when disabled people promote their rights as citizens, a right which is given prominence by the United Nations Declaration of the Rights for Disabled People (Oliver 1996). The process by which an individual's rights are represented may be called 'empowerment'.

Empowerment is about a process by which people gain control of their lives. To help people achieve a sense of empowerment professional workers should listen to those who experience a sense of powerlessness or vulnerability, and often this means disabled people, people from different ethnic groups, and women and children. The aim is to counteract the experience of ever-present powerlessness through membership of a disadvantaged group and to encourage confidence in one's ability to conduct one's own life. Social workers should help people to take control of their own lives by, for instance, by advocating on their client's behalf in making representations to health, education and welfare services about their need for services, support or advice. This is empowerment as self-advocatecy, but representation of others, as advocates, may be a necessary role for professionals.

The need for an advocate is exactly the situation of siblings: the danger is that adults are listened to first, and the needs of the disabled child second, leaving the situation of siblings, languishing in the background, as a final consideration, if considered at all, and indeed is represented by the experience of Mary, mentioned at the beginning of this chapter.

Empowerment also requires a cultural change within 'normal', as it might be expressed, 'non-disabled' society, as well as by those who consider themselves disabled. Disability carries its own stigma and is unconsciously accepted by some disabled people. While self-advocacy means being empowered oneself, one might question whether it is possible for people who do not have disabilities to help others. Perhaps self-help is not sufficient and there is a need to promote the acceptance and integration of disabled people and their families.

Research can benefit from ethnographic evidence that reflects and enriches in recounting the nature of personal relationships, and which will exclude any attempt to take over the individual's rights of expression, because they would then be subordinated to those of the observer and rendered meaningless. Indeed, the opposite should be the case, and in a professional sense workers need to encourage the right of self-expression as a way to determine individual needs, especially in situations where these have been denied.

The conception of disability without representation places families in an isolating experience with professionals needing to redress the balance by enabling families an accept their situation rather than rejecting it by neglecting to review their needs. The skill of self-help (Adams 1996) may be desirable, but many people require some professional help in the first instance to help recognise the difficulties they face and then in seeking help in dealing with the difficulties that are identified. Children and siblings of children with disabilities have a need to be understood: practitioners must communicate with children in order to understand these needs, because not to do so is a denial of their right to be involved in matters which concern them.

The need for empowerment: The child

The first question to be asked is why such a need arises in the first place. The medical model of disability can be used to illustrate how a disabled child may begin to be disempowered by the very nature of complex professional interactions which focus more on the disability than on the child concerned; and consequently social dependencies, particularly in the family, can lead to over-protection of the child, because he/she is seen as vulnerable. This perceived dependency might result in requests for professional involvement. Such concerns and their attendant responsibilities take their toll of each family member's ability to cope, a factor which, as Cairns (1992) acknowledges, will impact on the family in a number of ways.

Difficulties at home will, for example, cause parents to experience sleep disturbance, poor health and physical exhaustion. At such a point, the resulting involvement of professional agencies, whether social workers, community nurses or the education service, may help to eliminate any real sense of self-determination by the children. If there is no concerted effort to involve parents as well as children in discussions and decisions about health, education and other vital concerns, the experience of social exclusion leading to feelings of isolation and unimportance in family welfare. This is usually because many parents need attention in their own right and may be all too ready to allow someone else to take decisions for them, acquiescing in arrangements made on their and their child's behalf for what they believe to be the best. Siblings may learn to accept this as their only reaction to situations, leading to an acceptance of the inevitable neglect of their needs and a denial of their rights as individuals.

If, on the other hand, seeking professional help is viewed by carers, especially over-protective parents, as putting their child at risk (by, for example, encouraging a son or daughter to be more active in the community, use public transport and so on), then the parents may exercise their protective function by withdrawing permission to participate. Social work practitioners have to enable the persons to make choices while not ignoring parental involvement (Jackson and Jackson 1999). Thus, parental empowerment may be in competition with that of their children and with recommendations that carry professional authority; and the sense of partnership, which professionals strive to achieve, may suffer as a consequence. Again, the stepping order is downwards and with potential disagreements, siblings may find their needs, of all those being considered, the last to be realised.

When parents are over protective of their children and professionals need to take decisions in the disabled child's interest, parental and professional opinion may exclude a view from the child involved. One explanation might be that communication difficulties and problems with the child's expression of feelings might be cited for not including the child in the planning decision (Burke and Cigno 2001).

My view is that it would be foolish not to recognise that parents may speak ably for their children, but it would be equally wrong not to make every effort to communicate in whatever way possible with the children themselves, and children include not only those with disabilities but siblings too. It should not be a matter of competition either – of whose rights will be served; the rights of children should be in balance and equally considered, and when issues of child protection arise, the needs of the child come first.

Summary

In both research and practice, age and developmental factors are important. An adult, for example, has the duty and responsibility not to put a child or young person in a situation in which they cannot make informed decisions: a clear case is that of child sexual abuse, where the child cannot be said to give informed consent and where there is an imbalance of power and status.

In a daily practice context, professionals must be careful about the way that they phrase questions, making knowledge of child development and language crucial to their work. Sinclair (1996) and Hill (1998) consider how to involve children in decision-making, stressing the need to listen to what they say about services. Although they are writing about children in general, their work has clear relevance for disabled children. Bond (1999) reviews a pack specifically designed for children with learning difficulties to help them communicate their wishes and participate in service design. She stresses the necessity for creative and child-friendly tools and environments.

Agencies like the National Childrens Bureau, SCOPE and Mencap may act as representatives of young disabled people. However, the possible exploitation of disabled people by professionals, researchers and non-disabled people needs to be fully considered; non-disabled professionals should review the approach to their work that they adopt and be aware that the dissemination of information which concerns disabled people will affect those people's lives (Connors and Stalker 2003, p.27). Nevertheless, it would be difficult to argue that siblings of children with disabilities do not need concerned adults to help them make their needs and wishes known (Ward 1998; Ward and Simons, 1998). It is part of parental and professional responsibility to speak up for children, but to do so at the cost of excluding the child's viewpoint would essentially isolate the child further.

In the following case example, the experience of Rachel is compounded following a medical intervention which directs attention from her disabled sister, Susan, to herself. The sequence of events raises issues about possible causation which ultimately reflect on the difficulties which Rachel has to learn to handle.

The case of Rachel and Susan (high negative association)

Rachel, aged 14, has a younger sister Susan, aged 12, who has profound physical and intellectual disabilities. Susan attends a special school, requires one-to-one attention at all times and spends most of her time during the day in a purpose-built wheelchair. Susan is unable to feed herself and is fed via a tube directly into her stomach and, to add to her difficulties, she suffers from frequent epileptic fits. Rachel, a bright girl with a lively personality, attends a secondary school and helps with the care of Susan when at home.

Rachel spoke only of caring for Susan; there was no expression equivalent to 'playtime with Susan', an indication that Rachel was more conscious of 'a sense of duty to care' (my expression) than simply enjoying the company of her sister.

At the time of interview, Rachel had recovered from minor surgery to remove a lump from her neck, but some days after the operation she had experienced an 'epileptic fit' (as explained to her) which lasted about ten minutes. Rachel was taken to hospital and stayed for a period including overnight observation. She returned home only to find, some weeks later, that a similar thing happened again. The doctor indicated on the second occasion that the attack was likely to be of 'psychological origins' and not a true fit. Rachel was sent home and has had subsequent fits and experienced going to hospital on a regular basis as a consequence. Rachel has been prescribed medication to help control the fits, although an optimum balance appears yet to be determined and the fits continue on a regular basis.

Comment

The medical view appears to favour 'psychological' rather than a 'physiological' explanation for Rachel's fits. Rachel indicates that she feels she is being blamed for something she cannot control. Certainly, something changed after Rachel had minor surgery and unfortunately the medical reaction, as reported, would locate 'blame' as her problem. If the psychological explanation is accepted and the 'fit' is viewed as a reaction to stress or trauma, perhaps her difficulties are not a 'medical' condition in a psychological sense. This would clearly be a form of disability by association, arising from the perception that emulating disability increases the attention gained. However, whatever the causation of Rachel's fits, and whether or not there is a medical acknowledgement that these are physiological in origins, the need for medication seems to offer some progress forward. Indeed such a need might enable Rachel to gain control of her 'psychological' difficulty. Perhaps there is an undetected physiological causation, but wherever the true explanation lies, Rachel is experiencing difficulties and needs help.

As a sibling of a severely disabled sister Rachel might be viewed as someone seeking attention if the psychological explanation is accepted, and according to her behavioural indication her reactions could be considered as an expression of anger towards herself, linking to the concept of a negative overreaction to being the sibling of a severely disabled sister. The consequences of such a reaction can only be tested by enabling Rachel to gain the attention she needs in some other way: possibly by substituting her 'bad' experience with a more positively constructed one. Essentially Rachel needs more time for herself and more attention at home, and the latter should not always be directed through Susan.

The probability is that there is some element of both the psychological and physiological in Rachel's condition, and whether or not the fits are caused by some physiological dysfunction, perhaps as an unexpected consequence of surgery, the social element of the case, nevertheless, needs dealing with. Perhaps one-to-one attention, or involvement with a sibling group would help. Rachel needs to have her own identity reaffirmed as an individual in her own right, and to achieve this she may need professional assistance, irrespective of whether her fits are a result of surgery or a cry for help.

A need for assessment

I am concerned, also, following research into family support (Burke and Cigno 1996) that family attitudes towards a son or daughter with disabilities might result in a family becoming isolated from a community, which might otherwise support it. However, integration within the community depends largely on how the family adjusts to dealing with childhood disabilities, and in doing so professional help will be required to facilitate community involvement. Some families react to the experience of childhood disability by drawing away from the services that are available, making themselves increasing isolated, while others will welcome the attentions of specialist, voluntary services or neighbourly interest.

Recognising the variety of family characteristics is part of the assessment process required when providing assistance. The fear is that those who most need help do not seek it. The 'right' to be included might be suppressed by negative family attitudes, whether from pride, lack of acceptance or some form of desperation, but the effect is that the efforts of concerned professionals will be rejected.

Professionals must recognise that situations of neglect, where encountered, are within their remit to protect and provide for, helping families to overcome their own resistance to change. Professionals should also understand that some families might need coaxing to receive the help they need. This might be because they believe they 'have to deal with their own problems' and view the seeking of assistance as an admission of failure.

The siblings of children with disabilities have then a double obstacle to overcome – the legacy of parental attitudes which might reject help when it is needed and the fact that a disabled child will, inevitably, tend to receive more attention from parents, leaving siblings as secondary carers, whose childhood will include some element of neglect. This is not true for all families but it is the experience of some, and within the scope of an assessment it is necessary to identify the needs of all family members. The needs of disabled children and siblings should be considered. Equally, the framework for practice (Department of Health, 2000a) will help the implementation of such an approach, but it has its limitations, for reasons that I shall explain.

The assessment framework

The assessment framework for practice (Department of Health 2000a) represents the needs of siblings within a three-sided assessment framework (Appendix A, p.89). This consists of (i) child's developmental needs, (ii) parenting capacity, and (iii) family and environmental factors. The framework is understandably child-focused within the family context, with the view that children must be assessed according to their needs. The difficulty is that siblings may not be singled out for assessment independently but are considered in part only, owing to the assessment of the child with disabilities or, indeed, the child 'in need'. Rather than allowing a degree of uncertainty to exist, it is necessary to include a fourth side to the assessment triangle, a new one to include siblings. Consequently, there should follow, '(iv) the needs of siblings'. Siblings should be identified independently, to signify their role and importance within the family. The needs of the child with a disability will be considered independently but not separately from those of siblings, and both assessments should include a holistic view to reflect the situation of the family. This may be what most professionals will attempt, as part of good practice, when assessing a family situation, except, to repeat the point, the needs of siblings are not made sufficiently clear within the framework. It may be stating the obvious to express this omission; nevertheless, it needs this degree of clarification if siblings are not to risk a form of professional exclusion.

Power and independence

Empowerment requires a cultural change of view within 'normal' non-disabled society as well as a proactive form of help for people who consider themselves disabled. Disability carries its own stigma, sometimes accepted by people with disabilities themselves: the need is to view disability as a positive attribute within the mainstream of society.

Gaining control of one's own life is a basic right we all share and, as Oliver (1990) argues, the person who is disabled is the best person to describe what their needs are. Self-empowerment enables that process, as disabled children articulate their needs and, as they grow up, reject well-intentioned, pitying attitudes disguised as caring. Siblings are often caught up in this process, effectively experiencing disability in a secondary form, which will influence their views of their position in society; unfortunately, this will often carry 'the stigma' so frequently associated with disability in the past; in a literal sense, it is disability through a close relationship, becoming disabled by association.

The role of the professional is ambiguous, because the task of helping disabled individuals often denies their taking full responsibility for decisions, actions and choices. Parents can be ambivalent towards the professional, uncertain whether the professional is helping too little, causing frustration, or too much, causing them loss of face through poor 'image association' in managing their affairs. Similarly, the professional can be ambivalent, uncertain about the position of the disabled child in the decision-making forum.

Professional intervention and the need for research on its effectiveness need to clarify the shifting power base that the ambivalent response produces. Professional training must therefore include an examination of the need to empower disabled people rather than discriminating against them further through a lack of awareness, whether directly by non-communication, or in collusion with parents and others who presume to know what is best for them. If professionals do not act in the best interests of the child, they may be a potential danger to them, even though such action may be unintended (Burke 1999). However, to achieve the objective of putting the child first, it is first necessary to consider further the role played by informal carers in the empowerment equation.

The role of professionals and lay people alike is to recognise the right of people with disabilities and the need to promote policies and practice which directly include them. So far, most of the fact-finding and research in this area concerns adults (see, for example Oliver 1996). In the case of children, the focus has been mainly on the need for inclusive education policies, as exemplified by the journal *Inclusion*, although this same journal also covers articles on aspects of human rights and justice for disabled people internationally (Eigher 1998).

The needs of siblings are caught up in the expression of their 'rights', but may lie dormant due to the pressing needs of the disabled sibling and its parents: to ignore siblings is likely to produce problems at some stage in their lives. The situation of Rachel mentioned earlier (see p.113) highlights the divide that results, on the one hand, in an equable adjustment to life as a sibling of a child with disabilities or, on the other, in an experience which type-cast a disabling role for oneself. The latter, perhaps, representing a traumatic reaction to the disabling experience of surgery (in Rachel's experience) which raise difficulties that are not only of a physiological origin but appear to demonstrate that social and psychological difficulties too promote a sense of disability by association.

Chapter 9

Conclusions

Reflections on Professional Practice for Sibling and Family Support

Children need to be assessed within the family context, but professionals must also work in partnership with parents. This is difficult when the child's interests diverge from that of the parents, although professional assessments should always place the child's needs first. Barr (1999) indicates that relationships with professionals are built on successful early contacts and have a lasting impact on the ability of a family to adapt. Schreiber (1984) points to the importance of a holistic approach when working with the family – which is, as Gambrill (1983) expresses it, an ecological assessment, where the whole family is considered within their home environment. Risk factors, where siblings are concerned, should also be identified. The difficulty of balancing different needs according to Dale (1996) will occur when undertaking assessments, but may be overcome by allowing time to listen to each member of the family and ensuring that individual's needs are recorded.

It was somewhat unfortunate that a recent report on the Looked After Children, produced by the Health Select Committee (Modernising Social Services 2003, http://www.archive.official-document.co.uk/cm41/4169/chpa-3.htm) concluded that,

> standards of delivery and achievement are unreliable, and although many children benefit from social services, too many are let down.

Clearly the need is to raise standards in childcare for children in need and active support is needed from those with the power to influence service provision. As has been mentioned, 'Sure Start' (2003) has had a limited impact on the needs of disabled children and none on the needs of siblings, so proactive professional involvement is clearly required.

Powell and Ogle (1985) found that siblings have many concerns about their disabled brother or sister, about their parents and themselves. They consider that siblings have intense feelings and, in common with their parents, have many unanswered questions. Siblings need to talk to someone about their experiences, fears and feelings and a professional worker within a sibling group may help by enabling discussion group focus on the fears and tribulations of everyday life. Where there are only two children in the family, one source of sharing thoughts is unavailable (Murray and Jampolsky 1982) when the disabled child has severe difficulties, and the sibling group provides a healthy substitute based on common experiences.

It would be an error to assume that professional help is needed in all cases where siblings are concerned. Such a stance is potentially oppressive. Practitioners need to be sensitive to siblings' self-strategies, as demonstrated by the reactions listed in Table 2.1, and that choice is an essential part of an assessment. Nevertheless, siblings do need special consideration, for while adjustments may well be made in the family home, sibling experiences away from home, at school or elsewhere will be potentially testing for them. Moreover, as has been pointed out, siblings may be slow to share their worries with their parents. Care taken to obtain a clear picture of family relationships will reveal where there are differences in opinion held by family members (Sloper and Turner 1992). Consequently support services need to be offered with sensitivity, and family stress will be reduced – a view which informed Utting's (1995) report on preventing family breakdown.

Young carers

A recurring theme throughout this book has been that, when parents spend more of their time in dealing with the needs of a child with disabilities, brothers and sisters will receive less attention from them. It should also be clear that siblings will also be more likely to be called upon to perform parent surrogate roles, acting as secondary carers to enable parents to be relieved of some of the stresses associated with their primary caring responsibilities. McHale and Gamble (1987) found that girl siblings could be the most stressed because they were more likely to be expected to carry out such responsibilities than were boys. Sisters, particularly older sisters, according to Lobato (1983) are likely to be expected to undertake child-sitting and domestic work, while Sourkes (1990) indicates that they may be resentful of their parents' time being directed to their disabled brother or sister. These findings may, of course, be indicative of gender and age differences in the amount of household and caring responsibilities carried out by girls and boys (and later by men and women: see Evandrou 1990; Hubert 1991).

Thompson (1995) is concerned that young carers are denied their childhood by the nature of their caring responsibilities and stresses their need for support and counselling, as does Becker *et al.* (1998), who look at the strategy of helping young carers as a unique group as well as through support for the whole family.

It is apparent, therefore, that children do undertake adult roles for which they are ill prepared by definition of their youth. The Department of Health (1999), in a report on carers, and the earlier Carers (Recognition and Services) Act 1995 have reinforced the need to place greater emphasis on support and resources to avoid statutory intervention in families where young carers take on the main caring responsibility. This need is especially important for families where there is a child with disabilities, because an element of risk must exist when an immature individual attempts tasks beyond their ability to manage, no matter how determined that young person might be. However, all support needs are not the same, and may vary according to the nature of a child's disability, whether physical or of an intellectual kind (see Burke and Cigno 1996; Randall and Parker 1999) and on the family's own ability to help itself. I have shown that families and siblings vary in their ability to care, represented by Table 2.1 and Tables 4.1 to 4.3, so professionals must recognise the individuality of personal needs. Becker *et al.* (1998) convey the urgency of the plight of young carers, concluding that they represent a major area for preventive social-work interventions.

Medical and social models of disability

The sense that the medical world is concerned with diagnosis and treatment does not augur well for those whose condition is not curable. The pathology of a medical condition, in a sense, overtakes the human condition, and the discussion of need concerns health states and symptoms rather than the individual. To a large extent this is inevitable. It would be foolish to maintain that doctors and professions allied to medicine do not have an important part to play in the lives of disabled children or that medicine should not be about diagnosis and treatment: we all have need of these skills and knowledge at some point in our lives.

The social context, however, is crucial for the understanding of individual needs and social interactions. Medical conditions should not get in the way of attending to individual social needs. I therefore propose an integrated approach, essentially the best of both worlds, where medical need is properly recognised within the social context of living with learning disabilities. The balance between the medical and social has to be right. Recognising the contribution of different types of professional involvement helps that understanding. These issues are more easily addressed in multi-agency settings.

The medical model has elements of conveying powerlessness because those requiring treatment see doctors as possessors of powerful medical knowledge, and often unwittingly submit to a form of medical authority not always welcomed by doctors themselves. A multi-agency approach, especially where medical, educational and social welfare professionals work under one roof and undertake multidisciplinary assessments is, the evidence would suggest, the way forward.

The concept of exclusion brings with it ideas about its prevention. Exclusion can be avoided by introducing or amplifying networks of formal and informal care. Here, social welfare professionals aim to integrate families existing in isolation by providing the necessary support services and promoting self-advocacy and empowerment. The empowerment of siblings is aided by providing opportunities to discuss their feelings and experiences as a brother or sister of a disabled child. All too often, in the research that informs this book, siblings take a back seat in family matters, experience life as a compartment like existence and will at all times defend their disabled brother or sister, yet feel too respectful of parental views to express their feelings. Their situation is to appear as if disabled themselves, effectively disabled by association. The degree of such a disabling experience, represented by Table 2.1 in Chapter 2, suggests that reactions vary, each making the impact of disability somewhat different, but at whatever level, disability has a profound influence on their lives. This is often associated with increasing maturity, sensitivity and caring, but it also results in avoidance, reluctance to discuss matters that might offend and a suspicion that they may be in some way disabled too.

Similarities and differences

It is perhaps an obvious point that children represent our future: how we treat them will shape future experiences. Children with disabilities are children first and disabled children second. In adulthood the situation may become one of disability first if needs are denied and the social provision of services is neglected. This results in disability being viewed as a vehicle of oppression when, in reality, the situation of oppression will not occur if disabled people have their rights as full citizens upheld. In issues of social need, it can seem that the disability comes first, for it is necessary to draw attention to a child's unequal situation compared with other children. However, there is also a requirement for all children to be treated as children and future citizens without discrimination; otherwise the awareness of difference can be experienced as stigmatising.

Family life: Disability by association

Living in a family structure is a widely experienced phenomenon. The children within our families experience situations beyond the more 'ordinary' family experience: multi-professional and multi-agency contacts are not uncommon and, where uncoordinated, can be oppressive and confusing to consumers. Severely disabled children and their families are more likely to know about respite foster care, time spend in hostels, hospitals, even hospices for children with short life expectancies, so that their family life has special features. The family itself and the experience associated with disability service may come to feel 'disabled', since others often participate in managing their daily routines over their lifespan. Support is a fundamental need for families when they are coping with stress and disruption, which form part of everyday living. Support is more often provided within the family, although informal care is enhanced when supplemented by professional services. Siblings growing up with disability may then experience a sense of disability by association, as they become known as the brother or sister of a disabled child, a fact some, as I have indicated, may conceal from school friends in an attempt to follow a 'normal' life. Such experiences are unfortunately a reflection of the unequal status attributed to disability and essentially a greater integration of children with disabilities may help to educate other children and reduce the stigma of disability. Unfortunately, the structural inequality imposed by adherence to a medical model will perpetuate the sense of disability and its associations, in reaffirming a sense of being different. The social imperative is to redress the lot of disability and like race, cultural and gender issues, insights are slow in coming and slower when attempting to implement attitudinal change.

Children's needs

The needs of disabled children and siblings are not identical with those of parents, particularly as children grow up and begin to express their feelings. Although the views of family members may be similar, they are not coterminous. For instance, the parent's perspective is qualified by their experience and role while the child's is necessarily more intuitive and malleable. The needs of siblings vary and need to be taken into account, for they may need special help to enable them to manage the differences they perceive in their role and opportunities compared with their friends. Their futures also merit consideration. Children need to know at a basic level that disability is not contagious or dangerous, so that they will see the person first, otherwise the experience of social exclusion will be reinforced for the child with learning disabilities.

Assessments

Social workers should appreciate that each individual has different needs and that the family as a unit has needs which may be different for each of its members. I note that an assessment of family needs will often result in conflicting views, which do not have a ready solution. Professionals and families alike experience an ambivalent impulse about the quality and quantity of services: satisfaction and dissatisfaction can exist simultaneously. The way forward is to listen carefully to how families express their needs and to negotiate the way forward. It is important to have enough knowledge and information to be able to answer parents' questions on their child's development and care. Again, holistic assessments need at the very least a multidisciplinary approach, and I refer the reader to the account of its strengths and weaknesses within a multi-agency centre (Burke and Cigno 2000, p.122).

It requires professionals to become involved with siblings, to be able to recognise need at both emotional and practical levels, together with the implications for service provision. A goal at one point may change to another, as need itself varies, and may be articulated differently as circumstances change. The process of assessment should be subject to monitoring and review, rightly part of management enquiry, to enable an evaluation or re-evaluation of the assessment and intervention undertaken with the client (see Sutton and Herbert's (1992) ASPIRE model). However, as Middleton (1996) is keen to point out, assessment is not the resolution of the problem; it is the intervention that follows which is important.

Vulnerability and empowerment

Professionals will often understandably concentrate on vulnerability, as a concept particularly applicable to children with disabilities, who will, despite the loving care undertaken by most families, be more at risk of neglect and abuse. The balance to be achieved in working with families where there is a child in need is a delicate one. Empowering the vulnerable requires active involvement and a desire to improve the social standing and assertiveness of the individual. A child who is vulnerable is more at risk if isolated without extended family support, friends, contacts or professional help. Siblings experience a sense of deferred vulnerability if their disabled brothers or sisters are perceived as needing additional help with their daily routines. The daily interactions between siblings reinforce the sense of difference compared with their peers, as has been illustrated time and again within this book, although the positive side of this awareness is a developing resilience and adaptability to changed circumstances which will serve siblings well in later life. The knowledge that there is, however, a choice over many stages of the life course is empowering and increases self-esteem.

The final arbiter of adjustment is whether families as a whole are able to accept their lot, and accommodate their lives to the special needs of their disabled child. Brothers and sisters have to make adjustments and, as has been demonstrated, are a major help to their parents; they will grow up to face life differently. It will not be possible to be positive all the time about living with disability, but if carers are helped by their support networks, and demonstrate a degree of hopefulness, then their child with disabilities will be able to overcome the social barriers and obstacles which they will certainly encounter.

The future

Siblings of children with disabilities have something in common. They may not have discussed their thoughts, worries, or their future plans concerning their disabled brother or sister with their parents, nor do they want their parents to know that they have been thinking about the future. This is partly to do with protecting their parent's feelings, for brothers and sisters do not want to discuss with their parents the subject of old age, death, and the future of the disabled child.

All the siblings interviewed in the research were thinking about the future prospects of their disabled brother or sister; it is the one major feature they all had in common. However, all the parents interviewed, were, like myself, more concerned with daily events, often caused by tiredness and an inability to think about the long-term consequences of caring for a disabled child. If siblings were able to discuss their concerns with their parents, what they expressed were, for the most part, views concerning how they might help to reduce some of the pressures within their family.

Those siblings who have made a lifelong commitment to care for their disabled brother or sister did not show any emotion when speaking of their decision. It seemed a matter-of-fact situation but one which should be their responsibility and clearly their 'right' to follow their own life course is one which professionals might need to encourage. This perception is typified by the following extract, taken from an interview with a sibling (from Burke and Montgomery 2003):

> If Jamie's around when Mum and Dad die he'll come and live with me. If I'm able there's no way he'll go into residential care. I've accepted that since I was old enough to think.

> Graeme, aged 16

Such a view demonstrates that siblings need to be included within family discussions about current and future events. The research on which this book is based supports the evidence from Dyson (1996) who suggested that siblings will lose confidence and experience a sense of lowered self-esteem if they are not included in family discussion and their concerns aired.

There is, therefore, no conclusion to an ongoing process because the need for help continues through each and every transition that siblings face, which will often be on their own, and occasionally with family support. The practitioner must prepare for periods when input will be intensive and focused at times on child–parent interaction or specific problems to do with behavioural difficulties, manifested through an inability to deal with situations where only time and maturity can provide a solution to the difficulties experienced. The sibling support group is one way of helping siblings and has proved to be successful for the siblings commenting on its use in this research. However, in most circumstances the increase and variety of service provision needs to reflect the ebb and flow of everyday family life.

Chapter 10

Postscript

The research had ended and I made a presentation on the findings to an international conference – my research and the available evidence clearly suggested to me that disability by association was an established fact. I had the evidence I sought and the case examples necessary for this book. However, as part of this particular conference I had added on a family holiday for my partner, daughter and son (confined to his wheelchair), so we all went to a prestigious conference location. We were going to enjoy our holiday some several thousand miles away from home.

Two experiences on the conference holiday helped confirm my view that disability is really a family matter when one member is disabled. The first experience was on arrival at a hotel after an exhausting flight, only to find that despite booking ahead, declaring our wheelchair access needs (and being reassured that a lift was available to all floors, although we had reserved a ground floor room), we found that the room required the ascent of a dozen steps up, then down to get to our room. In the morning the same climb and descent had to be followed to access the dining area. The available lifts were not accessible by a ramp and also required several steps to be climbed to get to the lift doors, carrying the wheelchair with my son belted-in. The conference was on the needs of children, and my presentation was on the needs of disabled children and their siblings, but unfortunately, the conference arrangements did not live up to provisions for those with disabilities locally. However, my representation to the conference organising committee (who had recommended the hotel) succeeded and we were relocated to a more suitable and luxurious hotel at no additional cost.

The second experience was on the return flight to England. We had to have assistance in getting our son's wheelchair up and down the aisle on entering the aircraft. So, before landing I had requested that wheelchair assistance should be available. Much to our surprise, after the aircraft landed, we found four wheelchairs had been ordered and were awaiting our 'disabled family'. I often picture in my mind all four of us rolling through customs in wheelchairs; this really confirmed that disability by association, in its incremental and inexorable way, is as much a practicality of life for siblings, as indeed it is for the whole family.

Questionnaire
Support for Brothers
and Sisters of Disabled Children

	Variable Number
Questionnaire **Support for Brothers and Sisters** **of Disabled Children**	

Questionnaire
number

Please complete as many questions as possible.
Your answers will be treated in the strictest of confidence.

Questions about your child who has a disability   _____

1. Child's age (____years)   2. Child's sex   Male ☐
                                                       Female ☐
                                                       (tick box)

3. Please state the name or nature of your child's   _____
   disability:

4. Was the condition know to you at birth?   Yes ☐ No ☐

                                                             _____

   If no, how old was your child when you realised   _____
   he/she had a disability?

5. Who first told you about your child's condition _____
   (even if only suspected)?

6. Your experience of bringing up a disabled child will
   in some ways be different, but in others similar to
   bringing up any child, could you comment on
   differences (a) and similarities (b).

(a) Please say how your disabled child's experience
    is different:

    at home   _____

    at school   _____

(b) Please say how you think their experience is similar:

    at home   _____

    at school   _____

Brothers and Sisters

7. What are the ages of your children who do not have
   disabilities?

Boys   Girls

_____   _____

8. Do you think your children have benefited, in any
   way, from having a disabled brother or sister?

   Yes ☐   No ☐   _____

   If yes, please state how they have benefited.   _____

9. Have your children been disadvantaged by having
   a disabled brother or sister?

   Yes ☐   No ☐   _____

   If yes, please say how you think they have been   _____
   disadvantaged.

10. Do your non-disabled children help you with the care
    of their disabled brother or sister?

    Yes ☐   No ☐   _____

If yes, please say what they do. _____

11. Have your children ever expressed regret at having a disabled brother or sister?

Yes ☐   No ☐   _____

If yes, please say how he or she expresses this concern   _____

12. Do you think that your non-disabled children's leisure time is restricted in any way?

Yes ☐   No ☐   _____

If yes, please state how their leisure time has been restricted.   _____

13. What activities, additional to school attendance, do your children participate in?

Child 1 (with a disability)   _____

Child 2   _____

Child 3   _____

If you have more than three children please add any other children, plus activity here.

14. Are there any activities that brothers and sisters have not been able to follow (because of restrictions that having a disabled child may impose on the family)?

Yes ☐   No ☐   _____

If yes, please explain.   _____

15. Have any of the following people been involved in advising you about your children?

Please indicate by a tick the approximate frequency of contact.

	Disabled child						Non-disabled child					
	Once a						Once a					
Period	week	2 wks	month	3 mths	year		week	2 wks	month	3 mths	year	
Relative	☐	☐	☐	☐	☐	_____	☐	☐	☐	☐	☐	_____
Friend	☐	☐	☐	☐	☐	_____	☐	☐	☐	☐	☐	_____
Neighbour	☐	☐	☐	☐	☐	_____	☐	☐	☐	☐	☐	_____
Teacher	☐	☐	☐	☐	☐	_____	☐	☐	☐	☐	☐	_____
Social Worker	☐	☐	☐	☐	☐	_____	☐	☐	☐	☐	☐	_____
G.P.	☐	☐	☐	☐	☐	_____	☐	☐	☐	☐	☐	_____
Nurse	☐	☐	☐	☐	☐	_____	☐	☐	☐	☐	☐	_____
Psychologist	☐	☐	☐	☐	☐	_____	☐	☐	☐	☐	☐	_____
Counsellor	☐	☐	☐	☐	☐	_____	☐	☐	☐	☐	☐	_____
Group worker	☐	☐	☐	☐	☐	_____	☐	☐	☐	☐	☐	_____
Sitter service	☐	☐	☐	☐	☐	_____	☐	☐	☐	☐	☐	_____
Respite care	☐	☐	☐	☐	☐	_____	☐	☐	☐	☐	☐	_____
Other (please name)												
....	☐	☐	☐	☐	☐	_____	☐	☐	☐	☐	☐	_____
....	☐	☐	☐	☐	☐	_____	☐	☐	☐	☐	☐	_____

Of those people who have advised you (as ticked above) who were the most helpful?

1st ....   2nd ....

_____   _____

How were they helpful?   _____

16. Do your non-disabled children attend a Siblings
Support Group?   Yes ☐ No ☐

If yes, please name the group.   _____

Please show how helpful you feel this service to be
(circle one of the following numbers).

1 very helpful   2 fairly helpful   3 not very helpful   4 not at all helpful

_____

About You

17. Do you think your life would be very different if you   Yes ☐ No ☐
did not have a disabled child?
                                                    _____

If yes, how do you think you life would be different?   _____

18. What positive benefits has having a child with
disabilities brought to your family?   _____

19. Are you or your partner (if applicable) in paid   Yes ☐ No ☐
employment?
                                                    _____

If yes, what work do you/they do?

Self....................................   _____

Partner ....   _____

20. Would you agree to being interviewed (after returning   Yes ☐ No ☐
this questionnaire)?
                                                    _____

21. In the near future we would like to interview a number
of brothers and sisters about their experience of living
with a disabled child.

Would you agree to your non-disabled children being
interviewed (probably at home) about the experience of
having a disabled brother or sister?   Yes ☐ No ☐

_____

(We would not expect to interview any children under the age of 8 years.)

It would be very helpful to have a contact name and telephone number, if agreeing with questions 19 or 20 or both.

Name ....

Address ....

....

....

Telephone ....

Please indicate if you would like a report on our findings: Yes ☐ No ☐
                                                                _____

We would welcome any further comments you may have.

Thank you very much for your cooperation

Peter Burke
Sue Montgomery
University of Hull

Questionnaire
Sibling Group Evaluation

Siblings group evaluation (questionnaire distributed to group leader)

Ask:

What each person liked about the group

What each person would like more of

What each person would like to change

What improvements could be made

Whether sessions should be shorter, longer, more frequent

What continuity is needed when the series ends

Whether friendship groups have developed outside the set meetings

Siblings discussion

What is the best part of having a disabled sibling? ... the worst?

Do parents expect too much?

What do they expect?

Give examples of caring, playing, being involved with your brother/sister

Have you ever been embarrassed by your brother/sister? Give examples

School relationships

Have these been difficult as a result of having a disabled sibling? Give examples

Have you ever felt it difficult to bring friends home? Give examples of the difficulties

Do you feel you are any different from other young people because of your experience?
Give examples

Any other issues? (Ask each participant, i.e. individually going around the group).

Finally, ask a magic wand question. What would you most like to change to improve your life, if you had a magic wand (anything at all)?

References

Adams, R. (1996) *Social Work and Empowerment.* London: Macmillan.

Aldridge, J. and Becker, S. (1994) *A Friend Indeed: The Case for Befriending Young Carers.* Loughborough University: Young Carers Research Group.

Allot, S. (2001) 'Couldn't care more.' *Telegraph Magazine* (15 December) http://www.carersinformation.org.uk

ARC, The (2000) http://www.thearc.org/faqs/siblings.html

Atkinson, N. and Crawford, M. (1995) *All in the Family: Siblings and Disability,* London: NCH Action for Children.

Atkinson, R. L., Atkinson, R. C., Smith, E. E., Bem, D. J. and Hilgard, E. R. (1990) *Introduction to Psychology,* Tenth Edition. Orlando FL: Harcourt Brace Jovanovich.

Bank, S. and Kahn, M. (1982) *The Sibling Bond.* New York: Basic Books.

Barr, H. (1999) 'Genetic counselling: a consideration for the potential and key obstacles to assisting parents adapting to a child with learning disabilities.' *British Journal of Learning Disabilities 17*, 30–36.

Becker, S. (ed) (1995) *Young Carers in Europe: An Exploratory Cross-National Study in Britain, France, Sweden and Germany.* Loughborough University: Young Carers Research Group in association with the European Research Centre.

Becker, S. (2000) 'Carers (Young Carers).' *Research Matters,* Oct 1999 – April 2000. http://www.carersinformation.org.uk/showdoc.ihtml?id=625.

Becker, S. (2000) 'Carers – (Whole family approach to care).' *Research Matters,* April – Oct 2000. http://www.carersinformation.org.uk/showdoc.ihtml?id=576.

Becker, S., Aldridge, J. and Dearden, D. (1998) *Young Carers and their Families.* Oxford: Blackwell Science.

Beresford, B. (1994) 'Support from Services.' In *Positively Parents: Caring for a Severely Disabled Child.* London: HMSO.

Beresford, B. (1997) *Personal Accounts: Involving Disabled Children in Research.* The Stationery Office, Norwich: Social Policy Research Unit.

Blackard, M. K. and Barsch, E. T. (1982) 'Parents' and professionals' perceptions of the handicapped child's impact on the family.' *Journal of the Association of the Severely Handicapped 7*, 62–72.

Bond, H. (1999) 'Difficult transitions.' *Community Care,* 29 July–4 August.

Bone, M. and Meltzer, H. (1989) *The Prevalence of Disability Among Children.* London: HMSO. Office of Population Censuses and Surveys.

Bowlby, J. (1951) *Maternal Care and Mental Health.* Geneva: WHO.

Bradshaw, Y. W. (1993) 'The political economy of human need.' *Contemporary Sociology 22*, 77–88.

Bridge, G. (1999) *Parents as Care Managers.* Aldershot: Ashgate.

Brindle, D. (1998) 'Young Carers "Suffer Alone".' *Guardian*, 6 May.

Burke, P. (1993) 'Oppressive practices and child disability'. In G. Bradley and K. Wilson (eds) *The State, the Family and the Child,* University of Hull: Hull

Burke, P. (1998) 'Children with severe learning disabilities.' In K. Cigno and D. Bourn (eds) *Cognitive-Behavioural Social Work Practice.* Aldershot: Arena.

Burke, P. and Cigno, K. (1996) *Support for Families: Helping Children with Learning Disabilities.* Aldershot: Ashgate.

Burke, P. and Cigno, K. (2000) *Learning Disabilities in Children.* Oxford: Blackwell Science.

Burke, P. and Cigno, K. (2001) 'Communicating with Children with Learning Disabilities: Recognising the Need for Inclusive Practices.' *Journal of Child Centred Practice 6*, 2, 115–126.

Burke, P. and Montgomery, S. (2000) 'Siblings of children with disabilities: a pilot study.' *Journal of Learning Disability 4,* 3, 227–236.

Burke, P. and Montgomery, S. (2001a) 'Brothers and Sisters: supporting the siblings of children with disabilities.' *Practice, Journal of the British Association of Social Workers 13*, 1, 25–34.

Burke, P. and Montgomery, S. (2001b) *Finding a Voice, Supporting the Brothers and Sisters of Children with Disabilities. A Research Report Published for the Children's Research Fund.* Hull: University of Hull.

Burke, P. and Montgomery, S. (2003) *Finding a Voice.* Birmingham: BASW Expanding Horizons Series.

Busfield, J. (1987) 'Parenting and parenthood.' In G. Cohen (ed) *Policy is Personal: Sex Gender and Informal Care.* London: Tavistock.

Cairns, I. (1992) 'The health of mothers and fathers with a child with a disability.' *Health Visitor 65*, 238–239.

Carers National Association (2002) http:www.carersinformation.org.uk.

Centre for Inclusive Education (2003) web page: http://inclusion.uvve.ac.uk/csie/unscolaw.htm.

Chamba, R., Ahmed, W. and Hirst, M. (1999) *On the edge: Minority ethnic families caring for a severely disabled child.* York: The Policy Press.

Cigno, K. and Bourn, D. (eds) (1998) *Cognitive-behavioural Social Work in Practice.* Aldershot: Ashgate.

Cigno, K. with Burke, P. (1997) 'Single mothers of children with learning disabilities: an undervalued group.' *Journal of Interprofessional Care 11*, 177–186.

Cleave, G. (2000) 'The Human Rights Act 1998 – How will it Affect Child Law in England and Wales?' *Child Abuse Review 9*, 394–402.

Closs, A. (1998) 'Quality of Life of Children and Young People with Serious Medical Conditions.' In C. Robinson and K. Stalker (eds) *Growing Up with Disability, Research Highlights in Social Work 34*. London: Jessica Kingsley Publishers

Coleman, S. V. (1990) 'The siblings of the retarded child: self-concept, deficit compensation, motivation and perceived parental behaviour.' *Dissertation Abstracts International 51*, 67–69.

Connors, C. and Stalker, K. (2003) *The Views and Experiences of Disabled Children and Their Siblings: A Positive Outlook*. London: Jessica Kingsley Publishers.

Contact a Family (1998) *Siblings and Special Needs Fact Sheet*. London: Contact a Family. http://www.cafamily.org.uk/siblings.html.

Corbetta, P. (2003) *Social Research*. London: Sage Publications.

Corey, G. (2004) *Theory and Practice of Group Counselling*. Edn 6. Belmont NY: Thomson Brooks/Cole.

Crabtree, H. and Warner, L. (1999) *Too much to take on: a report on young carers and bullying*. London: The Princess Royal Trust for Carers.

Dale, N. (1996) *Working with Families with Special Needs: Partnership and Practice*. London: Routledge.

Dally, G. (1993) 'Familist ideology and possessive individualism.' In A. Beatie, M. Gott, L. Jones and M. Sidell (eds) *Health and Wellbeing*. London: Macmillan.

Daniel, B., Wassell, S. and Gilligan, R. (1999) *Child Development for Child Care and Protection Workers*. London: Jessica Kingsley Publishers.

Dearden, C. and Becker, S. (2000) 'Young Carers: Needs. Rights and Assessments' In J. Horwath (ed) *The Child's World: Assessing Children Needs, The Reader*. London: Department of Health.

Department of Education and Skills (2001) *The Code of Practice on the Identification and Assessment of Special Educational Needs*. London: The Stationery Office.

Department of Health (1991) *The Children Act 1989: Guidance and Regulations. Volume 6. Children with Disabilities: A New Framework for the Care and Upbringing of Children*. London: HMSO.

Department of Health (1998) *Modernising Social Services*. London: The Stationary Office.

Department of Health (1998) *Quality Protects: Framework for Action*. London: The Stationery Office.

Department of Health (1999) *Caring about Carers: A National Strategy for Carers*. London: The Stationery Office.

Department of Health (2000a) *Framework for the Assessment of Children in Need and their Families.* London: The Stationery Office.

Department of Health (2000b) *A Quality Strategy for Social Care.* London: The Stationery Office.

Department of Health (2001a) *Valuing People: A New Strategy for People with a Learning Disability.* London: The Stationery Office.

Department of Health (2001b) *Planning with People: Towards a Person Centred Approach – Guidance for the Implementation Group.* London: The Stationery Office.

Department of Health (2002) *Planning with People: Accessible Guide.* http://www.doh.gov.uk/ learningdisabilities/planning.htm.

Department of Health and Social Welfare (1986) *Mental Handicap: Patterns for Living.* Paper 555. Buckingham: Open University Press.

Disability Rights Commission (2003). http://www.drc-gb.org/drc/default.asp. http://www.drcgb.org/drc/InformationAndLegislation/NewsRelease_02 0904.asp.

Dowson, S. (1997) 'Empowerment Within Services: A Comfortable Delusion.' In P. Ramcharan, G. Roberts, G. Grant and J. Forland (eds) *Empowerment in Everyday Life.* London: Jessica Kingsley Publishers.

Dunn, J. and Kendrick, C. (1982) *Siblings: love, envy and understanding.* London: Grant McIntyre.

Dyson, L. (1996) 'The experience of families of children with learning disabilities: Parental stress, family functioning and sibling self-concept.' *Journal of Learning Disabilities 2,* 9, 280–286.

Eigher, W. (1998) 'Working towards human rights and social justice.' [Editorial] *Inclusion 20,* 1.

Evandrou, M. (1990) *Challenging the invisibility of carers: mapping informal care nationally.* Discussion Paper WSP/49. September. London: London School of Economics.

Finkelstein, V. (1993) 'Workbook 1: Being Disabled.' Milton Keynes: Open University Press.

Fitton, P. (1994) *Listen to Me: Communicating the Needs of People with Profound Intellectual and Multiple Disabilities.* London: Jessica Kingsley Publishers.

Fivush, R., Gray, J. T. and Fromhoff, F. A. (1987) 'Two-year olds talk about the past.' *Cognitive development 2,* 393–377.

Fonagy, P., Steele, M., Steele, H., Higgitt, A. and Target, M. (1994) 'The theory and practice of resilience'. *Journal of Child Psychology and Psychiatry 35,* 2, 231–57.

Frank, N. (1996) 'Helping families support siblings.' In P. J. Beckman (ed) *Strategies for Working with Families of Young Children with Disabilities.* Baltimore: Brookes Publishing Co.

Frank, N., Newcomb, S. and Beckman, P. J. (1996) 'Developing and Implementing Support Groups for Families.' In P. J. Beckman (ed) *Strategies for Working with Families of Young Children with Disabilities.* Baltimore: Brookes Publishing Co.

French, S. (1993) 'Can you see the rainbow? Roots of denial.' In J. Swain, Finkelstein, V., French, S. and Oliver, N. (eds) (1993) Disabling Barriers – Enabling Environments. London: Sage Publications/Open University.

Frude, N. (1991) *Understanding Family Problems: A Psychological Approach.* Chichester: Wiley and Sons.

Gambrill, E. (1983) *Casework: a Competency-based approach.* Englewood Cliffs: Prentice-Hall.

Gardner, A. and Smyle, S. R. (1997) 'How do we stop "doing" and start listening: responding to the emotional needs of people with learning disabilities.' *British Journal of Learning Disabilities 25,* 26–29.

Gath, A. (1990) 'Siblings of mentally retarded children.' *Midwife, Health Visitor and Community Nurse 26,* 4.

Gillespie-Sells, K. and Campbell, J. (1991) 'Disability Equality Training Guide.' Hertford: CCETSW.

Gilligan, R. (2001) 'Promoting Positive Outcomes for Children in Need: The Assessment of Protective Factors.' In J. Horwarth (ed) *The Child's World: Assessing Children in Need.* London: Jessica Kingsley Publishers.

Glendinning, C. (1986) *A Single Door: Social Work with the Families of Disabled Children.* London: Allen and Unwin.

Glazer, B. G. (1965) 'The Constant Comparative Method of Qualitative Analysis.' *Social Problems 12,* 436–45.

Goda, D. and Smeeton, N. (1993) 'Statistical considerations in Social Research.' *British Journal of Social Work 23,* 3, 277–281.

Grossman, F. (1972) *Brothers and Sisters of Retarded Children: An Exploratory Study.* New York: Syracuse University Press.

Herbert, M. (1993) *Working with Children and the Children Act.* Leicester: British Psychological Society.

Hill, M. (1998) 'What children and young people want from social services.' *Research, Policy and Planning 15,* 17–27.

Hopson, B. (1981) 'Transitions, understanding and managing personal change.' In M. Herbert (ed.) *Psychology for Social Workers.* London: Macmillan.

Horwitz, A. (1993) 'Siblings as Care Givers for the Seriously Mentally Ill.' *Milbank Quarterly.* http://www.carersinformation.org.uk/showdoc.ihtml /id=300.

Hubert, J. (1991) *Homebound: Crisis in the Care of Young People with Severe Learning Difficulties: A Story of 20 Families.* London: Kings Fund Centre.

Jackson, E. and Jackson, N. (1999) *Helping People with Learning Disability Explore Choice*. London: Jessica Kingsley Publishers.

Jenkinson, J. C. (1998) 'Parent choice in the education of students with disabilities.' *International Journal of Disability 45,* 189–202.

Jones, C. (1998) 'Early intervention: The eternal triangle'. In C.Robinson and K. Stalker (eds) *Growing Up with Disabilities*. London: Jessica Kingsley Publishers.

Joseph Rowntree Foundation (2003) http://www.jrf.org.uk/knowledge/findings/socialcare.

Kew, S. (1975) *Handicap and Family Crisis: A Study of the Siblings of Handicapped Children*. London: Pitman Publishing.

Knight, A. (1996) *Caring for a Disabled Child*. London: Straightforward Publishing Limited.

Kübler-Ross, E. (1969) *On Death and Dying*. London: Tavistock.

La Fontaine, J. (1991) *Bullying: The Child's View. An Analysis of Telephone Calls to Childline about Bullying*. London: Calouste Gulbenkian Foundation.

Law Commission (1995) *Mental Incapacity*. HMSO, London: Law Com. No. 231.

Lazarus, R. and Foulkman, S. (1984) *Stress, Appraisal, and Coping*. New York: Springer.

Lee, B. and de Majo, M. (1994) 'More strength than stress.' *Community Care,* 24 February, 5–6.

Lefcourt, H. M. (1976) *Locus of Control: Current Trends in Theory and Research*. Hillsborough, NJ: Lawrence Erlbaum.

Lobato, D. (1983) 'Siblings of handicapped children: a review.' *Journal of Autism and Development Disorders 13,* 347-364.

Lobato, D. (1990) *Brothers, Sisters and Special Needs*. Baltimore: Paul H. Brookes.

Loughborough University (2002) Annotated Bibliography provided by the Young Carers Research Group. Http://www.lboro.ac.uk/departments/ss/centers/YCRG/annotated.htm.

McCormack, M. A. (1978) *A Mentally Handicapped Child in the Family* . London: Constable.

McGurk, H. and Glachan, M. (1988) 'Children's conversation with adults.' *Children and Society 2,* 1,20–34.

McHale, H. and Gamble, W. C. (1987) 'The role of siblings and peers.' In J. Garbarino, P. E. Brookhauser and K. A. Authier (eds) *The Maltreatment of Children with Disabilities*. New York: Aldine de Gruyter.

Madden, P. (1988) 'A responsibility for life.' In *Community Care* 1 March.

Marks, D. (1999) *Disability: Controversial debates and psychological perspectives*. London: Routledge.

Marris, P. (1974) *Loss and Change*. London: Routledge and Kegan Paul.

Mayer, D. J. and Vadasy, P. F. (1997) *Sibshops: Workshop for Siblings of Children with Special Needs*. 2nd edn. Baltimore, MD: Paul H. Brooks.

Mayhew, K. and Munn, C. (1995) 'Siblings of children with special needs.' In *Child Care in Practice 2*, 1, 30–38.

Mayntz, R., Holm, K. and Hoebner, P. (1976) *Introducing Empirical Sociology.* Harmondsworth, Middx: Penguin Education.

Meadows, S. (1986) *Understanding Child Development.* London: Routledge.

Middleton, L. (1999) *Disabled Children: Challenging Social Exclusion.* Oxford: Blackwell Science.

Moeller, C. T. (1986) 'The effect of professionals on the family of a Handicapped Child.' In R. R. Fewell and P. F. Vadasy (eds) *Families of Handicapped Children: Needs and Supports Across The Life Span.* Austin, Texas: Pro-ed Inc.

Morris, J. (1998) *Don't leave us out: involving disabled children and young people with communication impairments.* York: YPS.

Morris, J. (2001) *That Kind of Life.* London: Scope.

Moser, C. A. and Kalton, G. (1971) *Survey Methods in Social Investigation.* London: Heinemann Educational Books.

Murray, G. and Jampolsky, G. G. (eds) (1982) *Straight from the Siblings: Another Look at the Rainbow.* Berkeley, CA: Celestial Arts.

Myers, R. (1978) *Like Normal People.* New York: McGraw-Hill.

Oliver, M. (1990) *The Politics of Disablement.* London: RKP.

Oliver, M. (1996) *Understanding Disability: From Theory to Practice.* Basingstoke: Macmillan.

Oppenheim, C. (1998) *An Inclusive Society: Strategies for Tackling Poverty.* London: Institute for Public Policy Research.

Parkes, C. (1975) *Bereavement: Studies of grief in adult life.* Harmondsworth, Middlesex: Penguin.

Pearlman, H. H. (1957) *Social Casework: A problem-solving process.* Chicago: University of Chicago Press.

Petr, C. and Barney, D. D. (1993) 'Reasonable efforts for children with disabilities: the parents' perspective.' *Social Work* 38, 247–255.

Philip, M. and Duckworth, D. (1982) *Children with Disabilities and their Families: A Review of Research.* Windsor: Nelson Publishing Company.

Phillips, R. (1998) 'Disabled Children in Permanent Substitute Families.' In C. Robinson and K. Stalker (eds) *Growing Up with Disability, Research Highlights in Social Work 34*, London: Jessica Kingsley Publishers.

Powell, T. and Gallagher, P. (1993) *Brothers and Sisters – a Special Part of Exceptional Families.* Baltimore: Brookes.

Powell, T. and Ogle, P. (1985) *Brothers and Sisters: A Special Part of Exceptional Families.* Baltimore: Brookes.

Quality Protects (2003) http://www.doh.gov.uk/qualityprotects/work_pro/project/work.

Randall, P. and Parker, J. (1999) *Supporting the Families of Children with Autism.* Chichester: Wiley.

Richardson, C. (1999) 'My sister, my life.' *Guardian* 3 November.

Rollins, M. (2002) CASS Young Carers Project. YC (leaflet) 15 http://www.carersinformation.org.uk/showdoc.ihtml?id=767.

Russell, P. (1997) *'Don't Forget Us.' Children with Learning Disabilities and Severe Challenging Behaviour.* Report of a Committee set up by The Mental Health Foundation. London: Mental Health Foundation.

Rutter, M. (1995) 'Resilience in the Face of Adversity: Protective Factors and Resistance to Psychiatric Disorder,' *British Journal of Psychiatry 147,* 598–611.

Schreiber, M. (1984) 'Normal siblings of retarded persons.' *Social Caseworker: the Journal of Contemporary Social Work 65,* 420–427.

Seligman, M. (1991) *The Family With a Handicapped Child: Understanding and Treatment,* 2nd edn. New York: Grune and Stratton.

Seligman, M. and Darling, R. B. (1989) *Ordinary Families, Special Children.* New York: Guildford Press.

Shakespeare, T. and Watson, N. (1998) *'Theoretical Perspectives on Research with Disabled Children.* In C. Robinson and K. Stalker (eds) (1998) *Growing up with disability.* London: Jessica Kingsley Publishers.

Sharkey, P. (2000) 'The Essentials of Community Care: A Guide for Practitioners.' Basingstoke: Macmillan.

Shaw, R. (1997) 'Services for Asian families and children with disabilities.' *Child Care, Health and Development 23,* 1, 41–6.

Siegal, B. and Silverstein, S. (1994) *What About Me? Growing Up With a Developmentally Disabled Sibling.* New York: Plenum Press.

Sinclair, R. (1996) 'Children's and young people's participation in decision-making: the legal framework in social services and education.' In M. Hill and J. Aldgate (eds) *Child Welfare Services: Developments in Law, Policy, Practice and Research.* London: Jessica Kingsley Publishers.

Sloper, P. and Turner, S. (1992) 'Service needs of families of children with severe disabilities.' *Child Care, Health and Development 18,* 259–282.

Smith, H. (1975) *Strategies for Social Research: The Methodological Imagination,* London: Prentice Hall.

Smith, J. (2002) *Listening, Hearing and Responding, Department of Health Action Plan: core principles for the involvement of children and young people.* Department of Health, 20 June. [http://www.doh.gov.uk/scg/actionplaninvolveyoung 2002.htm].

Social Exclusion Unit (2003) http://www.socialexclusionunit.gov.uk.

Social Services Inspectorate (1996) *Young Carers – Making a Start: Report of the SSI fieldwork project on families with disabilities or illness.* London: Department of Health/HMSO, October 1995 – January 1996.

Sone, K. (1993) 'Sibling support.' *Community Care.* 23 September.

Sourkes, B. (1990) 'Siblings count too.' *Candelighters, Childhood Cancer Foundation Youth Newsletter 12*, 6.

Sure Start (2003) http://www.surestart.gov.uk/news.

Sutton, C. (1994) *Social Work, Community Work and Psychology.* Leicester: British Psychological Society.

Sutton, C. and Herbert, M. (1992) *Mental Health: A Client Support Resource Pack.* London: NFER-Nelson.

Swain, J., Finkelstein, V., French, S. and Oliver, N. (eds) (1993) *Disabling Barriers – Enabling Environments.* London: Sage Publications/Open University.

Tait, T. and Beattie, A. (2001) *An evaluation of a pilot project for children with complex needs in Leicester, Leicestershire and Rutland.* Leicester: Mary Seacole Research Centre, De Montfort University, February.

Tanner, K. and Turney, D. (2000) 'The Role of Observation in the Assessment of Child Neglect.' *Child Abuse Review 9,. 337–348*

The Family Fund Trust (2003) http://www.jrf.org.uk/knowledge/findings/socialcare.

Thompson, A. (1995) 'Paradise Lost'. *Community Care, 25–31* May, 5.

Tozer, R. (1996) 'My brother's keeper? Sustaining sibling support.' *Health and Social Care in the Community 4*, 3, 177–181.

Tozer, R. (1999) *At the double: Supporting families with two or more severely disabled children.* London: National Children's Bureau.

Turney, D. (2000) 'The feminising of neglect.' *Child and Family Social Work 5,* 47–56.

United Nations (1989) *The Convention on the Rights of the Child.* Geneva: United Nations Children Fund.

Utting, W. (1995) *Family and Parenthood: Supporting Families, Preventing Breakdown.* York: Joseph Rowntree Foundation.

Wallace, W. (1995) 'Living with Disability.' *Nursery World,* March, 8–9.

Ward, L. (ed) (1998) *Innovations in Advocacy and Empowerment for People with Intellectual Difficulties.* London: Lisieux Hall.

Ward, L. and Simons, K. (1998) 'Practising partnership: involving people with learning difficulties in research.' *British Journal of Learning Disabilities 26,* 128–131.

Watson, J. (1991) 'The Queen.' *Down Syndrome News 15*, 108.

Weatherup, K. (1991) 'Family matters: siblings.' *Search (Muscular dystrophy group), 11*, 8–11.

Welch, M. (1998) 'Whose needs are we meeting?' *Professional Social Work*, 6 September.

Werner, E. (1990) 'Protective Factors and Individual Resilience.' In S. Meisels and J. Shonkoff (eds) *Handbook of Early Childhood Interventions.* Cambridge: University Press.

Williams, M. (2003) *Making Sense of Social Research.* London: Sage Publications.

Wilton, T. (2000) *Sexualities in Health and Social Care.* Buckingham: Open University Press.

Wolfensberger, W. (1998) *A Brief Introduction to Social Role Valorization: A High-order Concept for Addressing the Plight of Socially Devalued People, and for Structuring Human Services* (3rd edn). New York: Syracuse University.

Worden, W. (1991) *Grief counselling and grief therapy: A handbook for the mental health practitioner.* London: Routledge.

Subject Index

acceptance, as bereavement stage 32, 33
adaptive identity 77
ADHD (attention deficit hyperactivity disorder) 56
adjusting to transitional stages 80
adjustment stage 33
aggressive behaviour 45
analysis, framework for 29–40
anger, as bereavement stage 32, 33
ARC 97
Asians 56
assessment(s) 125
    framework 116
    need for 115
at-risk families 62
attachments 78–9
attitudinal barriers, changing 17
autism 63, 71, 87

babies 42–3
behaviours, reactive 33
bereavement, stages in 31–4
Black disabled people 22, 56, 58
Britain 15, 68, 69, 98, 107
bullying 74

Captain Hook 11
Carers National Association 67
Carers (Recognition and Services) Act 1995 121
caring responsibilities 59, 69–70
case histories
    Alan and Mary (compliant reaction) 88
    Daniel and brothers (compliant behaviour) 63–4
    comment 64
    David 64

Joe and Daniel 63–4
Fay and Michael 73–4
    locus of control 74
    positive over-reactive behaviour 74
Harry and brothers 49–50
    comment 50–1
    Douglas and Harry (high negative reaction) 50
    John, James and Harry (low negative reaction) 50
Jane and Richard 47–8
    comment 48–9
Peter and Ian (low negative reaction) 93
Rachel and Susan (high negative association) 113
    comment 113–14
Rani and Ahmed (high negative reaction) 56–7
    comment 57
Robert and Henry (high positive reaction) 82–3
Victoria, Jenny and Paul (low positive reaction) 86–8
change 77–80
child interviews 36
Children's Act 1989 108
children's needs 124
Children's Research Fund 14
classification of family types, developing 30–4
    locus of control 30–1
    stages in bereavement 31–4
cognitive-behavioural therapy 30
cognitive development, impact of disability during child's 46–7
communication and children's rights 107–8
communicating needs 106–7
community interaction 26
compliant behaviour 33, 63–4, 88
control
    group 38–9
    locus of 30–1

co-ordination, poor 81
culture 22

data analysis 39–40
defence mechanisms 80
denial 79
    as bereavement stage 32, 33
depression, as bereavement stage 32
developmental delay 43
diagnosis 21
difference 12, 26, 44
dignity, right to 15
disability
    by association 26–7, 34, 122–3
        diagram 26
    identifying integrated model of
        20–2
    impact on family 41–52
    models of 17–20
    and siblings 13–15
Disability Rights Commission 16
disease model of disability 22
displacement 79

embarrassment 84–5
empowerment 25–6
    need for: the child 110–12
    and role of professional 108–10
    and support services 105–18
    and vulnerability 125–6
epilepsy 49
ethnic groups 55–6
Europe 68
exclusion, social 24
exploitation of children, danger of
    in conducting research 36
external locus of control 33

face validity, establishing 40
family
    contact with formal and informal
        social networks 60

impact of disability on 41–52
    during child's cognitive
        development 46–7
    new child 42–3
    on being told your child is
        disabled/different 43–4
    sibling rivalry 45–6
    interviews 38
    living: disability by association
        122–3
    members, finding time for 65–6
    and sibling support 53–66
    and social experience 26
    stress 51–2
    support, need for 32
    types, developing classification of
        30–4
Family Fund Trust 51
Finding a Voice: Supporting the Brothers
    and Sisters of Children with
    Disabilities (Burke and
    Montgomery) 14
fighting 64
fits 113–14
fixation 32
Framework for the Assessment of Children
    in Need and Their Families (DoH)
    15
France 69

Germany 69
girl siblings, more stressed than boys
    121
grief reactions 32
group support 57–63
    how often? 100–1
    initial stress on joining 95–7
    role of 91–103
    what about parental
        responsibilities? 101–2
    what age groups? 99
    what kind of activities? 99–100
    what siblings liked about group
        experiences 97–8

who should attend? 98–9
growing up more quickly 68–9
guilt, as bereavement stage 32, 33

health practitioners 20–1
Health Select Committee 119
hearing impairment 47
heart condition 47
Holmes and Rage social adjustment
     scale 78
House of Lords 15

image association 11–12
inclusion 25
incontinence 47
independence and power 116–18
Independent Education Advisory
     Service 57
individualism and rights 15–18
infant, disabled 42–3
integrated model of disability
     how it translates to siblings 22–5
identifying 20–2
intellectualisation 79
interaction, community 26
internal locus of control 33
interviews 36

jealousy 45
Joseph Rowntree Foundation 11, 80

learning disability 73
     severe 88
life restrictions 72–3
lifts for wheelchair access 19, 129
locus of control 30–1, 33, 74
Looked After Children report (HSC)
     119
loss, sense of 26
Loughborough University 68

medical model of disability 17–20,
     122–3
medication 56
Mencap 21, 112
microcephaly 49
mobility difficulties 47
multi-agency approach to care and
     support 122
Muslims 56

National Children's Bureau 112
National Health Services and
     Community Care Act 1990 107
NCH Action for Children 72
needs, communicating 106–7
negative association, high 113
negative reaction 33, 50, 56–7
     high 50, 56–7
     low 50, 93
neglect 23–4, 26, 115
non-significant data 35

OPCS survey 53

parental interviews 36
parental responsibilities 101–2
parental views of benefits of having a
     disabled child compared with
     their perceptions of siblings'
     caring responsibilities 59
parents, relieving stress experienced
     by 70–2
person-centred approach 20, 22
Peter Pan (Barrie) 11
physical disability 93
pilot questionnaire 37–8
pilot stage of research 36, 37
positive over-reactive behaviour 74
positive reactions/responses 33, 86
     high 82–3
     low 86–8
power and independence 116–18

practice and theory 11–27
professional, role of and
    empowerment 108–10, 117
professional intervention 26
professional involvement and service
    provision (for sibling group) 61
professional practice for sibling and
    family support 119–27
projection 79
protection as reaction to living with
    childhood disability 32, 33

Quality Protects: Framework for Action
    15, 55–6
Questionnaire: Sibling Group
    Evaluation 137–9
Questionnaire: Support for Brothers
    and Sisters of Disabled Children
    131–6

race 22
Rani 12
reaction formation 79
reactive behaviours 33
    mixed 49–50
repression 79
research
    design 34–40
    findings 68–9
    involving children 36
    stages in 37–40
        data analysis 39–40
        establishing face validity 40
        further research 40
resilience 81–2
Richard III 11
rights and individualism 15–17

school, problems at 73
Scope 21, 112
self-actualisation 26
self-expression, need for 95
sibling(s)

and disability 13–15
group evaluation 137–9
how integrated model of disability
    translates to 22–5
perceptions 12–13
rivalry 45–6
support
    and family 53–66
    groups, role of 91–103
as surrogate parents 72
Siblings Support Group 38
single parent households 51
social construct, disability as 16–17
social construction 21
social exclusion 24, 26
Social Exclusion Unit 24
social model of disability 17–22,
    122–3
social networks, contact with formal
    and informal 60
social workers 21
special needs, identification of 42
SPSS Release 4.0 39
statement of special educational needs
    56
stress 78–9
    experienced by parents, relieving
        70–2
    family 51–2
    initial, on joining group 95–7
support
    need for 91–3
    services and empowerment
        105–18
sibling
    and family 53–66
    professional practice for 119–27
    groups
        initial stress on joining 95–7
    role of 91–103
    what siblings liked about group
        experiences 97–8
Sure Start 55–6
Sweden 69

test-retest technique 39
theory and practice 11–27
transitional stages, adjusting to 80
typologies, construction of 29

uncertainty 43
Union of the Physically Impaired
Against Segregation (UPIAS) 17
United Nations Convention on the
Rights of the Child 15–16, 107
United Nations Declaration of the
Rights for Disabled People 109
United States 68

verbal dyspraxia 47
vulnerability and empowerment
125–6

weight gain 56
welfare professionals 25
wheelchair access 19, 129–30

young carers 26, 120–2
children as 67–75
definition of 67

Author Index

Adams, R. 110, 141
Aldridge, J. 141
Allott 69, 83, 141
ARC 141
Atkinson, N. 53, 66, 69, 72, 83, 141
Atkinson, R.C. 141
Atkinson, R.L. 30, 33, 78, 79, 141

Bank, S. 71, 141
Barney, D.D. 65, 147
Barr, H. 92, 119, 141
Barrie, J.M. 11
Barsch, E.T. 46, 141
Beattie, A. 149
Becker, S. 68, 69, 74, 121, 141, 143
Beckman, P.J. 92, 145
Bem, D.J. 141
Beresford, B. 36, 54, 141
Blackard, M.K. 46, 141
Blackstone, T. 15
Bond, H. 112, 141
Bone, M. 53, 142
Bourn, D. 142
Bowlby, J. 78, 142
Bradshaw, Y.W. 34, 142
Bridge, G. 44, 45, 142
Brindle, D. 68, 142
Burke 60, 105, 106, 107
Burke, P. 2, 13, 14, 15, 16, 21, 23,
    25, 29, 30, 32, 37, 41, 42, 45,
    47, 51, 53, 54, 57, 58, 59, 61,
    68, 70, 72, 73, 83, 89, 92, 95,
    111, 115, 117, 121, 127, 136,
    142, 143
Busfield, J. 42, 142

Cairns, I. 110, 142
Campbell, J. 18, 145

Carers National Association 142
Centre for Inclusive Education 16,
    142
Chamba, R. 58, 142
Cigno, K. 13, 21, 23, 25, 32, 41, 42,
    51, 53, 59, 60, 73, 89, 105,
    106, 107, 111, 115, 121, 142,
    143,
Cleave, G. 143
Closs, A. 143
Coleman, S.V. 45, 143
Connors, C. 54, 85, 105, 112, 143
Contact a Family 143
Corbetta, P. 37, 38, 39, 143
Corey, G. 98, 143
Crabtree, H. 74, 143
Crawford, M. 53, 66, 69, 72, 83, 141

Dale, N. 119, 143
Dally, G. 143
Daniel, B. 143
Darling, R.B. 45, 148
de Majo, M. 62, 146
Dearden, C. 143
Dearden, D. 141
Department of Education and Skills
    56, 143
Department of Health 55, 69, 75,
    115, 116, 121, 143, 144
Department of Health and Social
    Welfare 144
Disability Rights Commission 144
Dowson, S. 25, 144
Duckworth, D. 54, 147
Dunn, J. 55, 144
Dyson, L. 82, 84, 127, 144

Eigher, W. 117, 144
Evandrou, M. 121, 144

Family Fund Trust 51, 149
Finkelstein, V. 109, 144, 149

Fitton, P. 106, 144
Fivush, R. 36, 144
Fonagy, P. 81, 144
Foulkman, S. 77, 146
Frank, N. 84, 92, 144, 145
French, S. 81, 82, 145, 149
Fromhoff, F.A. 144
Frude, N. 43, 46, 82, 91, 145

Gallagher, P. 69, 147
Gamble, W.C. 55, 121, 146
Gambrill, E. 119, 145
Gardner, A. 91, 145
Gath, A. 145
Gillespie-Sells, K. 18, 145
Gilligan, R. 81, 143, 145
Glachan, M. 36, 146
Glazer, B.G. 40, 145
Glendenning, C. 44, 53, 54, 55, 145
Goda, D. 35, 145
Gray, J.T. 144
Grossman, F. 69, 145

Herbert, M. 101, 125, 145, 149
Higgitt, A. 144
Hilgard, E.R. 141
Hill, M. 112, 145
Hoebner, P. 147
Holm, K. 147
Hopson, B. 51, 78, 79, 145
Horwitz, A. 68, 145
Hubert, J. 121, 145

Jackson, E. 146
Jackson, N. 146
Jampolsky, G.G. 120, 147
Jenkinson, J.C. 82, 146
Jones, C. 80, 146
Joseph Rowntree Foundation 80

Kahn, M. 71, 141
Kalton, G. 40, 147

Kendrick 55
Kendrick, C. 144
Kew, S. 45, 46, 146
Knight, A. 43, 146
Kübler-Ross, E. 31, 32, 33, 43, 146

La Fontaine, J. 74, 146
Law Commission 108, 146
Lazarus, R. 77, 146
Lee, B. 62, 146
Lefcourt, H.M. 30, 33, 146
Lobato, D. 46, 69, 121, 146

McCormack, M.A. 53, 146
McGurk, H. 36, 146
McHale, H. 55, 121, 146
Madden, P. 146
Marks, D. 22, 146
Marris, P. 65, 146
Mayer, D.J. 47, 146
Mayhew, K. 47, 70, 83, 147
Mayntz, R. 34, 147
Meadows, S. 31, 50, 55, 85, 147
Meltzer, H. 53, 142
Middleton, L. 24, 44, 77, 125, 147
Moeller, C.T. 42, 147
Montgomery, S. 14, 15, 16, 25, 29,
        37, 41, 42, 45, 48, 51, 53, 54,
        57, 58, 59, 61, 68, 70, 72, 83,
        92, 95, 127, 136, 142
Morris 24, 36
Morris, J. 147
Morris, Lord 15
Moser, C.A. 40, 147
Munn, C. 47, 70, 83, 147
Murray, G. 120, 147
Myers, R. 68, 147

Newcomb, S. 92, 145

Ogle, P. 46, 54, 66, 69, 72, 120, 147

Oliver, M. 17, 18, 19, 20, 23, 109, 116, 117, 147
Oliver, N. 149
Oppenheim, C. 24, 147

Parker, J. 121, 148
Parkes, C. 31, 147
Pearlman, H.H. 40, 147
Petr, C. 65, 147
Philip, M. 54, 147
Phillips, R. 12, 56, 147
Powell, T. 46, 54, 66, 69, 69, 72, 120, 147

Quality Protects 147

Randall, P. 121, 148
Richardson, C. 72, 84, 92, 148
Rollins, M. 67, 148
Russell, P. 43, 148
Rutter, M. 34, 78, 148

Schreiber, M. 119, 148
Seligman 45, 71, 72
Seligman, M. 148
Shakespeare, T. 13, 17, 22, 148
Shakespeare, W. 11
Sharkey, P. 25, 148
Shaw, R. 148
Siegal, B. 70, 148
Silverstein, S. 70, 148
Simons, K. 112, 149
Sinclair, R. 112, 148
Sloper, P. 120, 148
Smeeton, N. 35, 145
Smith, E.E. 141
Smith, H. 40, 148
Smith, J. 148
Smyle, S.R. 91, 145
Social Exclusion Unit 24, 148
Social Services Inspectorate 69, 148
Sone, K. 54, 59, 149

Sourkes, B. 121, 149
Stalker, K. 54, 85, 105, 112, 143
Steele, H. 144
Steele, M. 144
Sure Start 55, 120, 149
Sutton 125
Sutton, C. 50, 149
Swain, J. 18, 149

Tait, T. 149
Tanner, K. 23, 149
Target, M. 144
Thompson, A. 62, 66, 121, 149
Tozer, R. 57, 58, 70, 149
Turner, S. 120, 148
Turney, D. 23, 149

United Nations 149
Utting, W. 120, 149

Vadasy, P F. 47, 146

Wallace, W. 149
Ward, L. 112, 149
Warner, L. 74, 143
Wassell, S. 81, 143
Watson, J. 149
Watson, N. 13, 17, 22, 46, 148
Weatherup, K. 47, 149
Welch, M. 106, 149
Werner, E. 81, 150
Williams, M. 40, 150
Wilton, T. 22, 150
Wolfensberger, W. 11, 77, 150
Worden, W. 31, 150

Printed in the United Kingdom
by Lightning Source UK Ltd.
129511UK00002B/208-225/A